SIMPLY SEMINOLE

DOROTHY HANISKO

SIMPLY SEMINOLE

Techniques & Designs in Quilt Making

THE QUILT DIGEST PRESS
Simply the Best from NTC Publishing Group
Lincolnwood, Illinois U.S.A.

Editorial and production direction by Anne Knudsen.

Book and cover design by John Lyle Design, San Francisco.

Technical editing Kandy Petersen.

Technical drawings by Kandy Petersen.

Quilt photography by Sharon Risedorph, San Francisco.

Printed in China

Library of Congress Cataloging-in-Publication Data

Hanisko, Dorothy

  Simply Seminole : techniques and designs in quilt making / Dorothy Hanisko. — 1st ed.

  p. cm.

  ISBN 0-8442-2647-5 (pbk.)

  1. Patchwork—Patterns. 2. Patchwork quilts. 3. Seminole textile fabrics.

  4. Strip quilting. I. Title.

  TT835.H3358 1987

  746.46—dc20

Published by The Quilt Digest Press

a division of NTC/Contemporary Publishing Company

4255 West Touhy Avenue

Lincolnwood (Chicago), Illinois 60646-1975, U.S.A.

6 7 8 9 10 WKT 8 7 6 5

45" x 72" (114 cm x 183 cm)
From top: Syncopated Piano Keys variation (alternate);
Cross (alternate); Maze/Letter T (alternate);
Diamonds variation (angle); Rick-Rack (stairstep);
Syncopated Piano Keys (alternate); Box Kites (stairstep).

DEDICATION

To my husband, Chris, and sons, Eric and Will, for their
unending support and encouragement.

ACKNOWLEDGMENTS

Heartfelt thanks to

Celeste Alexander, Donna Ball, and Lauretta Ehling who
were there from the first. My students, whose creativity
and enthusiasm always provide inspiration and renewal.
All those who made bands and willingly shared their quilts.
Lassie Whitman, whose excellent class introduced me
to Seminole strip piecing. Anne Knudsen, for editorial
direction and guidance, the patience of a saint, and the
stamina of a long-distance runner. Kandy Petersen, for
drawings that make my instructions come to life.

My thanks also to Omnigrid, Burlington, WA, Quilt
Quarters, Port Angeles, WA, and Quilt with Ease, Everett,
WA, for quilting supplies. Special thanks to The Heard
Museum, Phoeniz, AZ, for allowing me access to its
collection of Seminole garments.

CONTENTS

INTRODUCTION

45" x 72" (114 cm x 183 cm)
Marilyn Welch, Port Angeles, WA
From top: Piano Keys variation (alternate);
Greek Cross (floating); Rick-Rack (stairstep);
Interlock (stairstep); Piano Keys (alternate).

An Exciting Quilting Form for Today's Quilters

Seminole patchwork is a perfect quilting style for today's quilters. This may come as a surprise, for Seminole, one of the most beautiful and intricate quilting forms, has always had a reputation for being time-consuming, even tedious. In *Simply Seminole*, we'll look at Seminole from a fresh perspective—a form of patchwork ideal for the busy, overextended quilter who is looking for stunning results in record time.

A Natural Transition into Quilting

When I first discovered Seminole as a beginning quilter, it was considered a technique best suited to smaller projects, especially garments. This is most likely because of its origins—it was used by the Native American Seminole of south Florida who developed it almost exclusively for embellishing clothing. I enjoyed making the bands and found the techniques I learned invaluable when I started drafting my own quilt patterns. But since my love was for making full quilts, my enthusiasm for Seminole soon waned. I found the bands awkward to integrate into my quilts and had no interest in smaller projects nor in wearable art.

As time passed, my fascination with Seminole quietly grew. Though I still did not care to make them myself, I was drawn to the designs I saw in Seminole garments. I saw in them an appeal that went beyond the beauty of the individual bands that, at last, I realized could be applied to every area of quilting. And by seeing the bands as part of a larger whole, the time it took to complete them did not seem quite as daunting as it once had. When I looked closely at the bands as they were used in Seminole garments, something amazing happened. I saw that the garments are not composed of intricate band upon intricate band, each striving to outdo the other. Usually, only four bands are contained in any one project, and, of those, only one or two are complex. These are simply placed between strips of fabric of varying width and color. The strips serve to maintain the rhythm of the design and repeat the colors used in the bands, without becoming a distraction. They provide a perfect setting to display the more intricate designs of the bands themselves. The overall effect is one of excitement and surprising simplicity. I realized the same technique can easily be transferred to making full quilts, limiting the time it takes to make them but achieving the same dramatic results.

Bold, Large-Scale Designs

One other variation from traditional Seminole made my conversion to this quilting form complete. While tiny one-inch-wide bands are appropriate in garments, they are easily lost in a full-size quilt. By simply adjusting the scale of the bands to the larger quilt size, the translation of Seminole from small projects to quilts works.

One of the most rewarding aspects of large-scale Seminole is close to the heart of all quilters. Traditionally, Seminole patchwork is done either in solids or in very small-scale prints so that the design is not obscured. Although solids have a lot to offer, we don't necessarily want to be limited to them. Making larger-scale bands opens the door to using any fabric desired. Even those that don't work well in the bands themselves can be effective as borders between them. The result is that we can use a dazzling array of fabrics and yet maintain a perfect harmony within a Seminole quilt.

Break Away from Block Quilts

Another rather obvious yet unique dimension of Seminole is that the long, narrow bands make a refreshing change from the typical square quilting block. Once I stopped trying to use bands in the same way that I had used blocks, a whole new world of quilt design opened up before me. Working with the bands instead of against them, I found that their strong, unwavering horizontal structure works perfectly in quilts, allowing for wonderful flexibility in design.

Quilts made from blocks are based on a grid structure. Blocks are interdependent. Without sashing, secondary patterns are formed between adjoining blocks, and so they must work well together. Even with sashing, block sizes must be compatible. Mixing blocks of varying sizes can be a drafting nightmare. Seminole bands, rather than being interdependent, are interrelated. Since they run parallel to each other, never touching, each is an independent, self-contained unit within the larger body of the quilt. Bands of varying height and pattern pose no drafting problems since each forms its own line across the quilt. This makes it possible to select an assortment of designs for the same quilt. Block quilts are usually limited to one or two.

Every quilter finds it difficult to choose between equally attractive patterns. With Seminole, we can pick as many patterns as we have bands. This allows a wonderful opportunity for self-expression, for creating that unique look. Bands can reflect personal taste and individuality, or, in quilts made as gifts, can be tailored to the tastes and personality of the recipient.

QUICK QUILT ASSEMBLY—STUNNING RESULTS IN RECORD TIME

The construction method in Seminole flows logically from the band format. Whereas in traditional patchwork the quilt top needs to be completed before assembly and quilting begin, in Seminole, all three stages happen at the same time. Bands are joined and quilted simultaneously. This ease of assembly makes it realistic to complete a quilt in as little as two days. Because Seminole demands less time and energy than other quilting forms, it's easier to be spontaneous. For most of us, it takes time even to get started on a quilt project. With Seminole, the ability to finish quickly allows us to give in to impulse and make quilts on a whim. This makes Seminole quilts the best kind of gift—one that is spontaneous and is all the more appreciated for being unexpected.

Seminole quilts are also wonderful gifts for those—like children and teenagers—who cannot be counted on to keep a quilt in mint condition. When a child loves a quilt, it is dragged around everywhere. It becomes part of the child's life. Although this is wonderful to see, it can be heartbreaking to watch hours of painstaking work acquire the patina of wear and tear that goes with this kind of devotion. Enter, Seminole quilts. The limited time expended makes the quilt no less loving a gift but allows a certain detachment.

USING *SIMPLY SEMINOLE*

In writing *Simply Seminole* I had three objectives. First, I wanted to teach the basics of strip piecing and provide a catalog of patterns that can be quickly and easily made up into quilts. Chapter 1 of *Simply Seminole* introduces the four key techniques that make up Seminole strip piecing and explains how each band type is made. Chapter 2 is a ready reference of basic sewing and quilting techniques, many valuable in all forms of quilting, and some particular to Seminole. If you run into any problems in making the bands, simply check here for the answers. My catalog of patterns, Chapters 4 to 7, provides patterns for making 36 different Seminole bands, all with step-by-step directions and detailed diagrams. In Chapter 8, there are complete instructions for assembling the bands into finished quilts.

Second, since the versatility of Seminole allows for endless experimentation, I wanted to include the basics of color and design that will allow both beginners and experienced quilters to build confidence in creating quilts that are unique to them. Chapter 3 explains the principles of design and explains how to achieve the dramatic, bold lines characteristic of Seminole through working in contrasting colors. You can also choose softer colors for more subtle effects. Chapter 3 also provides help on choosing from the vast array of fabrics available to achieve the look you are aiming for. Exercises help quilters to integrate theory into practice and experiment with pattern and color combinations of their own.

Third, by including photographs of beautiful, fine-quality quilts throughout the book, I hope to inspire you to reach for the very best that your skills and your imagination offer.

GLOSSARY

ALTERNATE BAND. The least difficult of Seminole bands to make, using only 90° cuts.

ANGLE BAND. Band whose segments are cut at a 45° angle and arranged either open or in mirrored pairs.

ASSEMBLY SET. Cluster of a band and two or more horizontal strips stitched together lengthwise as the first step in the assembly process.

BAND. Unit of several sections, stitched together forming the completed Seminole design.

FLOATING BAND. Band whose pieced sections are positioned next to unpieced spacers so that they appear to float.

HORIZONTAL STRIP. Plain strip of unpieced fabric that serves to separate the Seminole bands when assembling a quilt.

SECTION. Unit of several pieced segments stitched together, edge to edge.

SEGMENT. Slice of a strip set, cut either straight or on an angle, ready to be joined with other segments or with spacers.

SELVAGE. Finished edges of fabric, running lengthwise.

SEMINOLE STRIP PIECING. Style of decorative patchwork originating with the Seminole of south Florida in the early 1900s, now adapted to quilting.

SPACER. Unpieced strip of fabric used to separate two pieced units.

STAIRSTEP BAND. Band requiring only 90° cuts whose segments are joined in a staggered or offset pattern, then turned to form a diagonal design.

STRIP. Piece of fabric cut with the grain, generally selvage to selvage.

STRIP SET. Group of strips, stitched together lengthwise.

Strip set   Segment   Section   Section with spacers

Seminole band

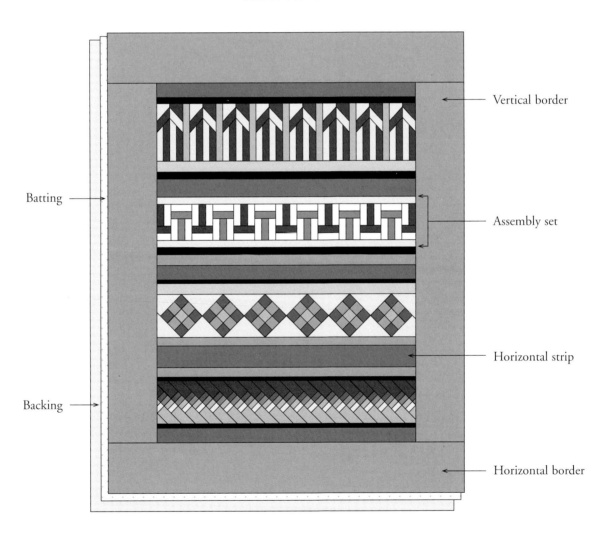

Vertical border

Batting

Assembly set

Backing

Horizontal strip

Horizontal border

The Making of a Seminole Quilt

SEMINOLE ESSENTIALS

Cutting mat

Rotary cutter

Clear rulers—12" x 24" (30cm x 60cm) plus 6" x 12" (15cm x 30cm)

Scissors

Sewing machine

Glass head quilting pins

Thread

Seam ripper

Chalk marker or marking pencil

Steam iron

Ironing board

THE BASICS

The excitement of Seminole strip piecing and the simplicity of its construction bring wonderful new opportunities to quilters. It is a perfect medium for beginning quilters who need quick results to keep them motivated and is equally well suited to the experienced quilter seeking new creative challenges.

The three chapters in Section One describe Seminole, explain the basic skills, and introduce color and design principles that help build confidence and inspire creativity. Use this section as a resource for practicing techniques and as a source of ideas as you work on the bands in Section Two.

45" x 72" (114 cm x 183 cm)
Celeste Alexander, Port Angeles, WA
From top: Criss-Cross (stairstep); Maze/Letter T (alternate);
Tumbling Cross (floating); Diamonds variation (angle);
Broken Chain variation (floating).

WHAT IS SEMINOLE?

Seminole strip piecing has its roots in a simple form of decorative patchwork created by the Native Americans of south Florida at the turn of the century. Passed on from generation to generation it is characterized by bold designs and bright combinations of color that belie the simplicity of the techniques behind them. Used by the Seminole to embellish dress, Seminole strip piecing has made a natural transition into the world of quilting.

HOW SEMINOLE STRIP PIECING WORKS

1. Fabric strips of a variety of widths, patterns, and colors are cut, then sewn back together and ironed to create a **strip set**.

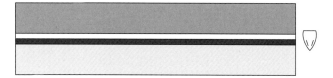

2. The strip sets are sliced into **segments**. The cuts can be either straight or angled, creating either straight or angled segments.

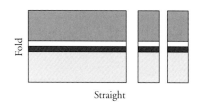

Straight

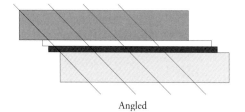

Angled

3. The segments are repositioned and sewn back together, edge to edge, to form **sections**.

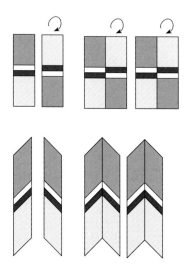

4. The sections are then stitched edge to edge to form completed **bands**. The bands are squared and trimmed, ready for assembly into quilts.

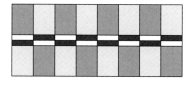

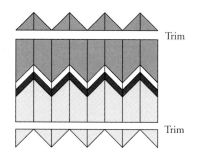

Trim

Trim

This illustrates just how easy Seminole strip piecing is.

The technique is as simple as it sounds, but the results can be astounding. By using multiple strips of fabrics cut and arranged in a variety of ways, quilters can build an endless array of patterns. Add color and the patterns jump to life.

Seminole work is an ideal form for today's quilters. Quick and easy, it offers the busy quilter rich opportunities for creativity and makes results possible in a day that otherwise would be relegated to "perhaps someday . . . ."

THE FOUR BASIC SEMINOLE BANDS

Simply Seminole offers quilters a catalog of 36 band designs from which to choose. These are organized into four key piecing techniques, from the most simple to the most complex.

1. Alternate bands
2. Stairstep bands
3. Floating bands
4. Angled bands—mirror and open angles

These groupings help you understand and practice the basic principles of Seminole, by emphasizing the similarities of each technique rather than their differences. Once you start creating your own variations, the groupings are even more useful and help you remember how you created each new effect.

The quilt on page 11 uses all four band types. There are just four steps to making each one. Let's take a closer look at how each is achieved.

MAKING ALTERNATE BANDS

The simplest Seminole form, alternate bands are modest and unassuming. Nonetheless, they offer a wealth of possibilities. Their very simplicity provides a welcome counterpoint to the more elaborate bands used in the same quilt.

Alternate bands involve the least difficult construction techniques in Seminole work, making them an ideal choice for beginner quilters. The following diagrams demonstrate the simple, four-step process through which the bands are made.

STRIP SET. Cut strips of fabric and stitch lengthwise into sets.

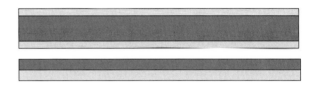

SEGMENTS. Slice the strip sets into segments.

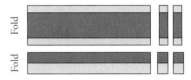

SECTIONS. Stitch the segments edge to edge to form sections. Three variations are possible. You can alternate a segment from one strip set with a segment from another made from different fabrics. You can alternate an unpieced spacer strip. Or you can flip every second segment (turn it upside down). It's even easy to combine all three techniques into the same section.

Segments may alternate with one or more spacer strips.

Alternate segments may be flipped to from a pattern.

13

Segments may alternate with segments from a different set.

Segments may alternate with segments from a different set *and* with a spacer strip.

BAND. Stitch the sections edge to edge, matching the seamlines, to form a band. Trim.

Note that all cuts are at right angles, making the segments very easy to piece back together. This also means that making alternate bands provides beginners with an excellent opportunity for mastering skills in rotary cutting. And although precise matches are always desirable, alternate bands are the most forgiving of Seminole forms, producing stunning results even when seam allowances vary a little more than they should.

Because of their simplicity, alternate bands allow more experienced quilters a perfect medium through which to experiment with color. Free from technical concerns, the quilter can concentrate completely on color and fabric choices with dazzling effects. Both for the experienced quilter seeking new challenges and for the novice, then, alternate bands are by far the best place to begin. In Chapter 4, there are ten different patterns for alternate bands.

MAKING STAIRSTEP BANDS

Though the results can look quite complex, stairstep bands are deceptively easy to make. They are constructed in much the same way as alternate bands. Like alternate bands, all the cuts are straight—there are no angle cuts to make. Once cut, the segments are simply stitched back together in stairstep pattern. So great is the transformation that it's hard to envision the finished band by viewing the beginning stages. The diagrams illustrate the process.

STRIP SET. Cut strips of fabric and stitch lengthwise into sets.

SEGMENTS. Slice the sets into segments.

SECTIONS. Stitch in a stairstep pattern, matching seamlines, to create sections.

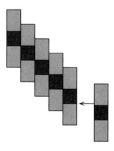

BAND. To complete the band without waste, simply slice through the section and rejoin at the opposite end, matching seamlines. Both ends will now be square.

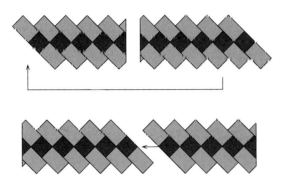

Trim the edges to form the band.

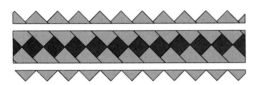

As well as adding stunning accents to any quilt, stairstep bands can be used to create such intriguing patterns that they can easily stand alone. Although more challenging than alternate bands, the techniques are easily mastered by the beginner and can be endlessly adapted into myriad variations by the more experienced quilter.

In Chapter 5, there are six different patterns for stairstep bands.

MAKING FLOATING BANDS

Floating bands are created by placing pieced sections between diagonally cut spacers, so that they appear to float. Floating bands are characteristic of the very best qualities of Seminole patchwork. Once you master one simple technique, the possibilities are endless. Their beauty is matched only by the ease with which they are made. The diagrams show how this is done.

STRIP SET. Cut strips of fabric and stitch lengthwise into sets. Cut a strip of spacer fabric.

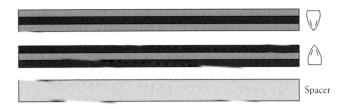

SEGMENTS. Slice the sets and the spacer into segments.

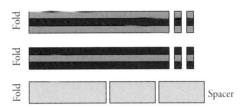

SECTIONS. Stitch the set segments edge to edge to form sections. Stitch the sections edge to edge with the spacers, alternating sections and spacers. Cut through the spacer at a 45° angle, equidistant between the seamlines.

BAND. Turn the sections on end and stitch edge to edge, matching seamlines. To complete the band without waste, simply slice through the section and rejoin at the opposite end, matching seamlines. Both ends will now be square. Trim the edges to form the band.

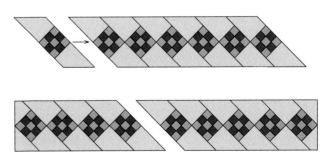

One wonderful quality of floating bands is their versatility. By changing the spacer fabric, the band can take on a wholly different look. Floating bands also give the quilter a chance to use scraps of a favorite fabric that are too small to be practical in other types of bands.

In Chapter 6, there are eight different patterns for floating bands.

MAKING ANGLE BANDS

The most challenging of all band types, the variety possible from using angle bands is astonishing. There are two types of angle bands–open angle and mirror angle. The techniques behind them, as demonstrated in the following diagrams, are identical.

STRIP SET. Cut strips of fabric and stitch lengthwise into staggered sets. For open angles, one staggered set is needed. For mirror angles, two staggered mirrored sets are needed.

SEGMENTS. Slice the sets at a 45° angle into segments. For open angles, all the segments are identical. For mirror angles, half the segments will be mirror images of the other half.

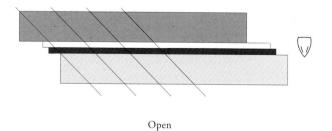

Open

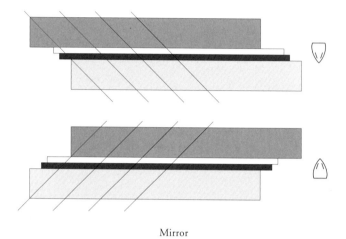

Mirror

SECTIONS. Stitch the segments together edge to edge. There are many ways to position them, depending on the desired effect.

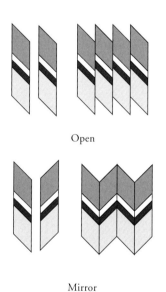

Open

Mirror

BAND. Stitch the sections edge to edge, matching seamlines, to form bands. Trim.

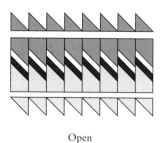

Open

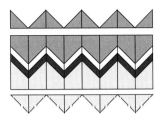

Mirror

Precision is important in making angled bands. All the pizzazz doesn't come without a price! Accuracy in measuring and cutting at a 45° angle is essential, and it takes practice. A quilters' ruler that shows angle marks is an invaluable tool, saving time and ensuring accuracy.

In Chapter 7, there are six different patterns for mirror-angle bands and six patterns for open-angle bands.

Chapter 2

READY REFERENCE—SKILLS FOR SEMINOLE

44" x 71" (112 cm x 180 cm)
From top: Diamonds (angle); Snail Trail (alternate);
Syncopated Piano Keys (alternate); Tumbling Fish (floating).

Using the Ready Reference

In this chapter, we explore the key skills that will allow you to create any Seminole design. You may want to skim the chapter before you start making bands, but its real purpose is to serve as a ready reference while you are working. For ease of use, the skills are grouped into those you will need for making strip sets, segments, sections, and bands. Whether you are new to quilting or new to Seminole, these guidelines will save time, increase accuracy, and perfect your sewing skills. If you run into difficulties making any of the bands, simply check here for the answers to your problems.

Preparing the Fabric

If you are new to quilting, I recommend prewashed cotton fabrics. As well as the wonderful feel of cotton, it irons beautifully, allowing seams to lie flat.

Prewash all fabrics, no matter how colorfast the manufacturer tells you they are. Don't risk spoiling your work by having the colors run the first time you wash your quilt. Prewash according to color groups in warm water, followed by a cool rinse. Some fabrics may need to be washed more than once. Note that reds and greens tend to run more frequently than other colors. For difficult fabrics, add vinegar to the rinse cycle. Tumble dry.

Skills for Making Strips

Rotary Cutting

Rotary cutting is ideal for Seminole. It's fast and accurate, and there's no need to premark the fabric. Rotary cutting allows you to make clean, crisp cuts through multiple layers of fabric. All you need is a rotary cutter, a clear ruler (6" x 24"/15 cm x 60 cm), a rotary cutting mat, and a flat surface.

1. All strips are cut selvage to selvage. For most standard fabrics, this is approximately 40" to 42" (102 cm to 107 cm).
2. Fold the fabric selvage to selvage and place on the cutting mat.
3. Position the ruler with the bulk of the fabric underneath it so that the fold aligns with a horizontal marking on the ruler. The fold aligns with the ruler's horizontal marking line.

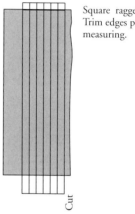

Square ragged edge. Trim edges prior to measuring.

Cut

4. Press firmly on the cutter, making a smooth cut away from yourself along the full length of the ruler. Reposition fabric so that the newly cut edge aligns with the selected measurement marking on the ruler.
5. Press firmly on the cutter, making a smooth cut away from yourself along the full length of the ruler.

Correct:

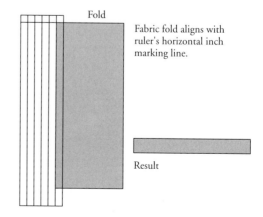

Fold

Fabric fold aligns with ruler's horizontal inch marking line.

Result

Incorrect:

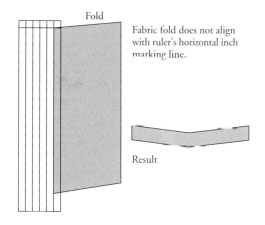

Fold

Fabric fold does not align with ruler's horizontal inch marking line.

Result

STITCHING

Because of slight differences in selvage-to-selvage measurements from fabric to fabric, not all your cut strips will be the same length. They may vary as much as two inches. As you sew them into strip sets, match all strips at one end.

Correct:

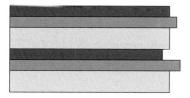

Incorrect:

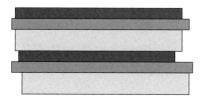

However, do not start sewing from that end for every seam, as you may get a rainbow effect—the entire set will curve slightly. Instead, sew from opposite ends for alternate seams.

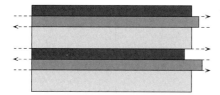

To complete the strip set, fold it in half and square up the ends with a ruler and rotary cutter to trim off the uneven edges.

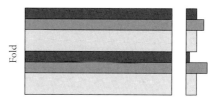

Fold

STITCHING STRIPS FOR ANGLE BANDS

When making strip sets for angle bands, this simple technique saves fabric. Rather than align all the strips at one end, stagger them as shown. Draw a chalkline at a 45° angle from the lower left corner of the bottom strip. Stitch the top strip, matching slightly to the left of the chalk mark. Repeat for the rest of the strips in the set.

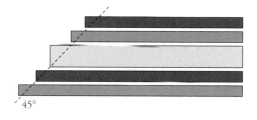

45°

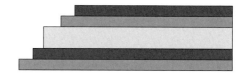

IRONING

To make the lines in strip sets crisp and perfectly parallel, it's important to make sure that no tucks or folds are hidden in the seamlines on the right side of the fabric. Using a hot steam iron, press firmly on the back of the fabric, pressing all seams in the same direction until the fabric lies completely flat. Turn the fabric over and iron again, this time from the opposite direction. This allows the iron to work into the seams, taking out even tiny wrinkles. Follow the iron icons on the band patterns to make sure you are pressing seams in the right direction. This is critical for accurate piecing.

SKILLS FOR MAKING SEGMENTS

CUTTING

To create clean, squared segments, position the ruler on top of the strip set so that the cut edge aligns with the correct measurement line. The seamline should align with the ruler's horizontal marking line. A 6" x 12" (15 cm x 30 cm) ruler is easy to manage. Make firm, smooth cuts away from yourself. You can cut two segments at a time simply by folding the strip set.

Correct: seamline aligns with ruler:

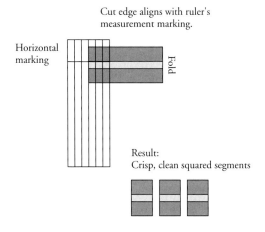

Cut edge aligns with ruler's measurement marking.

Horizontal marking

Fold

Result:
Crisp, clean squared segments

Incorrect: seamline does not align with ruler:

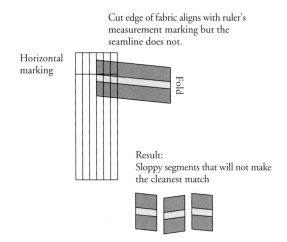

Cut edge of fabric aligns with ruler's measurement marking but the seamline does not.

Horizontal marking

Fold

Result:
Sloppy segments that will not make the cleanest match

CUTTING AT ANGLES

Quilters' rulers are marked with 30º, 45º, and 60º angles. Useful for all kinds of quilting, these are essential for creating the angle bands of Seminole. Lay the ruler over the fabric, matching the desired angle to a seamline, and the cut edge to the correct measurement. Cut cleanly and crisply using a rotary cutter. For accuracy, double-check the angle after cutting every two or three segments as you work across a strip set.

Cut to trim edges:

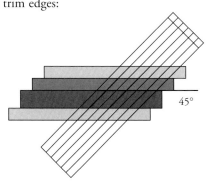

45°

Cut to measure:

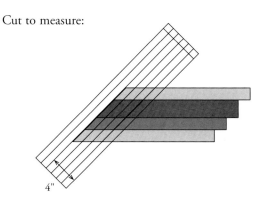

4"

USING SPACER STRIPS

Many Seminole designs alternate pieced segments with unpieced spacers. Here is a quick and easy way to create this effect. Rather than precutting, matching, and piecing the individual spacers, sew the pieced segments directly onto a long spacer strip. This not only helps maintain consistent placement, it also saves time. Particularly for beginning quilters, this technique allows a little latitude when, try as you might, seam allowances are not exactly a quarter inch.

IRONING

Once strip sets are cut into segments, they should require no further pressing.

SKILLS FOR MAKING SECTIONS

CHAIN PIECING

Chain piecing—feeding segments through the sewing machine in an unbroken line—saves time, thread, and frustration. Speeding up the process of sewing segments together, chain piecing also makes it easy to keep the many segments used in a typical Seminole band in the correct order.

Stitch:

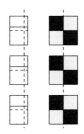

Snip and move:

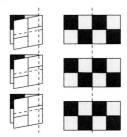

Snip and move:

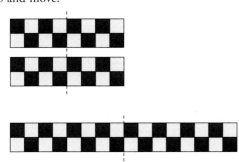

1. Match all the segments together into pairs, right sides together. Feed the first pair into the sewing machine, sewing down one side and a few extra stitches off the end. Feed in the next pair and repeat. Continue until all the pairs are connected, taking care not to break the connecting thread. You will have a chain of paired segments.

2. Without removing the chain from the machine, snip off the first two pairs you stitched. Open them out and rejoin to create a quad. Repeat until you have a chain of quads.

3. Repeat, joining quads, until there are just two long sections.

4. Snip the thread and stitch the two sections together to form a band.

MATCHING SEGMENTS IN ANGLE BANDS

The match when chain sewing Zig-Zag and Arrowhead is particularly tricky. To match 45° cuts like these to form a continuous line, place the segments right sides together, offset slightly as shown, and stitch so that the seam is at the intersection.

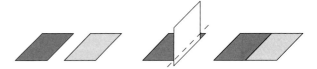

To match other 45° angle segments, simply match the seam allowance of the seamline in the first segment to the seam allowance of the seamline in the next. Stitch.

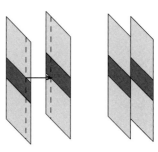

IRONING

Proper pressing procedures for sections will make a world of difference in the appearance of your band. The goal is to avoid excess bulk—seams stacking on top of one another—to the greatest extent possible. There are two key points to remember.

1. Interlock seams whenever possible. Seam allowance should fall in opposite directions in joined pairs of segments. This should happen naturally if you followed the iron icons on the diagrams. This is of particular importance for mirror angle bands.

2. When joining segments to spacers, press seam allowance toward spacer.

As many sections are likely to have bias edges and so stretch easily, keep pressing to a minimum. Press from the right side only, setting the iron down flat and using short, light strokes. Finger pressing or pinching works well with those stubborn seams that fall in the wrong direction. Quick and easy, finger pressing is less likely to stretch the fabric than ironing. It works particularly well with bias edging—ironing may not even be necessary.

SKILLS FOR MAKING BANDS

TRIMMING

Once the segments are joined into a continuous band, the edges must be trimmed to cut away irregularities and to make sure the top and bottom are parallel. Align a ruler with the seamlines to square up the edges and, using a rotary cutter, trim away uneven edges. Once trimmed, the band is smooth and even, ready for assembly into a quilt.

SQUARING OFF STAIRSTEP BANDS

Once the stairstep band is sewn together, turn it on its side so that the squares stand up on the points. Notice that at either end there will be wasted angled pieces. To maximize the usable band area, make a single slice straight up and down anywhere in the band—perhaps through a poorly matched piece—aligning the seamline with the 45° angle mark on the ruler. Now match and sew the two angled edges together. You will have a band with two square ends, without having wasted fabric.

To create straight edges along both sides of a stairstep band, all the little peaks or triangles of fabric must be neatly and accurately trimmed off, leaving a seam allowance of at least a quarter inch. Trim off the ragged edges carefully, four or five peaks at a time. Make sure the edges are parallel.

Sew all segments in stairstep pattern:

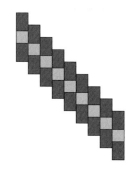

Turn unit so it stands on points:

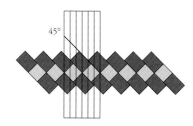

Make one slice. If a match is poor, slice at that point:

Move piece to opposite end, match and stitch:

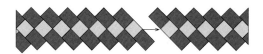

Trim edges. Leave seam allowance like this:

Not like this. Not enough seam allowance:

SQUARING OFF FLOATING BANDS

There are two ways of finishing floating bands.

1. The simplest method is to square them off in exactly the same way as stairstep bands—slice through the band at a right angle and match and sew the two angled edges together. This method is quick and effective, and wastes no fabric. There is a slight drawback, however, that becomes evident when you assemble your quilt. Notice how each end of the band now ends with the precise tip of a square. As you assemble the quilt, you may need to adjust the border so that it chops through the end of the square at one or both ends, giving the band an uneven look.

Slice:

Transfer:

Match and join:

2. This method of squaring off avoids the uneven look the first option causes. Once the sections are completely joined, rather than slicing and transferring, simply add a large half-square triangle of the spacer fabric to each end. This acts as a buffer, extending the band so that there is ample room to add the borders without interrupting the square pattern.

Square off:

SQUARING OFF OPEN-ANGLE BANDS

Open-angle bands are squared in exactly the same way as stairstep bands. Simply slice straight through the band, then match and sew the two angled edges together. You will have a band with two square ends, without having wasted fabric. Trim the edges parallel to each other.

Slice:

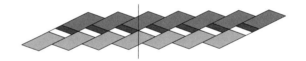

Transfer:

Match and trim:

IRONING

Press bands gently from the right side, with enough pressure to flatten, but without stretching the bias edges. Check that all matches are accurate. If they are not, before you rip the seam, try turning the band over and pressing the seam allowance to the opposite side. This may be just enough to even up the match.

Chapter 3

COLOR AND DESIGN—
A PERFECT PARTNERSHIP

45" x 72" (114 cm x 183 cm)
From top: Medallion/Letter I (alternate); Rattlesnake variation (floating);
Piano Keys (alternate); Crystals (angle); Snail Trail (alternate).

Quilting as Artistry

I believe the reason behind the enduring popularity of quilting is that it imbues everyday articles with a sense of artistry. Quilts serve not only as a means of providing warmth and comfort, but are, themselves, objects of beauty. Beginning quilters know from the start that they must learn to sew, yet it is only once they plan a quilt that they realize they must also become artists. This is all part of the joy of quilting. Learning Seminole piecing is no exception. You will learn technical skills that will allow you to work faster and achieve more polished results. But you will also learn the excitement of experimenting with design and working with color. For this, Seminole is the perfect medium. Its simplicity allows even those who lack confidence to develop an artistic sensibility that makes their Seminole quilts unique.

A Combination of Color and Pattern

What is it that makes you gaze on some quilts and want to wrap them around you, while you walk past others that are equally well crafted or stitched? What visual qualities do those exceptional quilt designs share? For me, that extra spark comes from the quilter's combination of color and pattern.

To be visually pleasing, the colors and patterns of a quilt must offer both a sense of unity and a feeling of variety. Unity allows the eye to see the quilt as a whole, no matter how many colors or patterns are crafted into it. The different sections of the quilt, dynamic or static, balance each other. The colors, whether they blend smoothly into each other or offer stark contrasts, work well together. The borders and bands are complementary. The overall impact is one of energy and diversity, yet completeness.

But how are effective combinations of color and pattern achieved? This is the question that worries most quilters. Lacking confidence in our own abilities, too many of us give up even before we start by approaching color and design with feelings of trepidation and defeat. The first and most important step in overcoming our fears is to realize that use of color and design is simply a skill to be developed like any other. Once you learn and practice a few important basics and understand your own likes and dislikes, color and pattern fall into place. Seminole, because you're working with small quantities of fabric and because of its technical simplicity, is a perfect practice ground—you can experiment in color and design no matter how little time, fabric, or energy you feel you have to spare.

To help explain how color and design work in quilts, I've selected three quilts with strikingly different color schemes and band patterns. The quilt on page 29 uses high-intensity, saturated colors, and a lot of black, with an effect that is reminiscent of color use in Amish quilts. In contrast, in the quilt on page 30, bright fuchsias and teals work together with an equally dramatic effect. In the quilt on page 31, the colors are soft and much lighter. As we work through some of the basics of color and design, these quilts will help show what happens when different combinations are used together.

Elements of Color

The best way to begin learning about color is to open your eyes and look around you. The world is full of color. From home decorations to fashions to magazines to nature itself, look at colors in everything you see and notice how they work together. Think not just about the primary colors but the teals, the maroons, the turquoises, the burgundies, and the peaches. See how they vary, how many colors are possible, and how they play off each other. At the same time, look carefully at the colors you see in quilts. Ask yourself what it is about

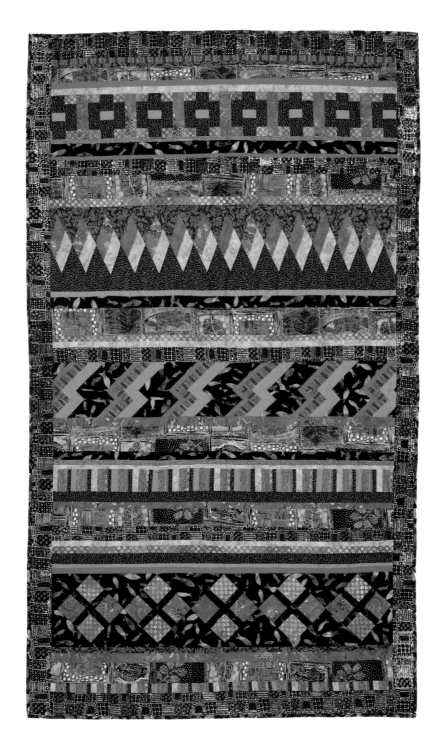

45" x 72" (114 cm x 183 cm)
From top: Medallion/Letter I (alternate); Diamonds (angle);
Zigzag (angle); Syncopated Piano Keys (alternate);
Rattlesnake (floating); Syncopated Piano Keys (alternate).

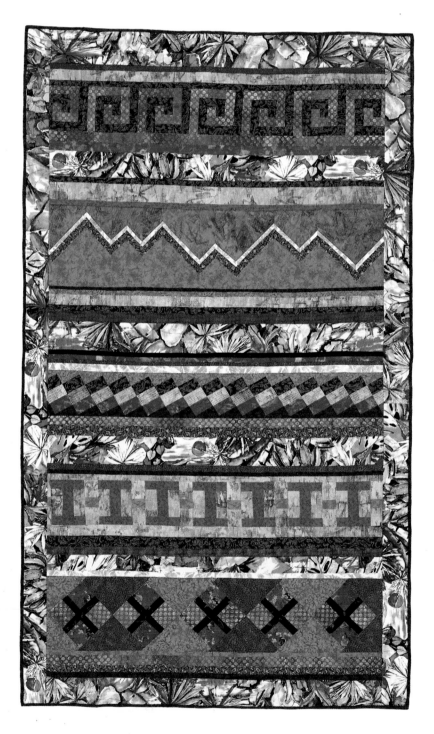

46" x 73" (117 cm x 185 cm)
From top: Snail Trail (alternate); Fraternal Peaks (angle);
Dominoes (stairstep); Medallion/Letter I (alternate);
Rattlesnake (floating).

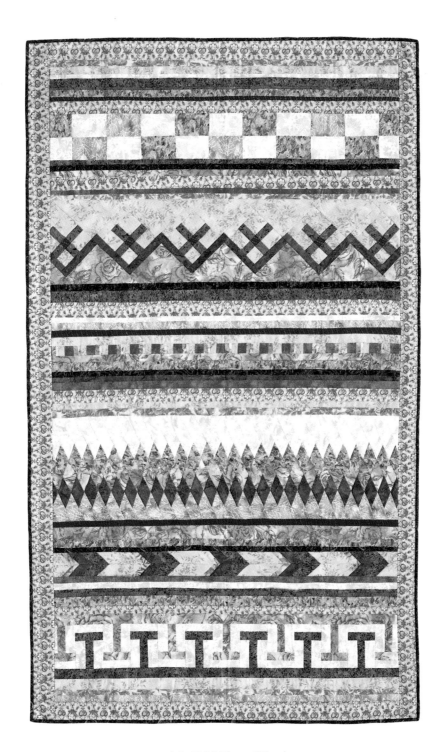

41" x 70" (104 cm x 178 cm)
From top: Checkerboard variation (alternate); Desert Flower
(floating); Syncopated Piano Keys variation (alternate);
Crystals (angle); Arrowhead (angle); Maze/Letter T (alternate).

color use you like or dislike. Compare the quilts you admire. Look for uses of color and special color effects that you can incorporate into quilts of your own. Spend time with fabrics and fabric swatches. Practice moving them around to create pleasing color combinations. As you work and find out more about your own preferences, keep notes and samples.

CLASSES OF COLORS

HUE

What is known as the color wheel is simply an arrangement of the spectrum of the twelve pure colors or hues of which all other gradations of color are made. The twelve hues fall into three color classes or categories: primary, secondary, and tertiary. Primary colors are those that cannot be created by mixing. The three primary colors are red, yellow, and blue. Secondary colors are those that can be created by mixing the primary colors:

RED + YELLOW = ORANGE
RED + BLUE = VIOLET
BLUE + YELLOW = GREEN

Tertiary colors are created by mixing a primary color and a secondary color. Red-orange, red-violet, yellow-green, yellow-orange, blue-green, and blue-violet are the tertiary colors. Beyond this, each pure color or hue can be produced in an endless range of intensities and values.

VALUE

The value of a color is the amount of light or dark in it.

Think of the color you are analyzing as on a spectrum from white to black. Lighter values are known as tints; darker values as shades. This band is made from a repeating pattern from dark to light. The eye is immediately drawn to light values, here set off by the black-patterned fabric.

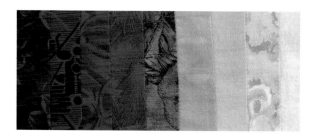

The colors in the quilt on page 31 are mostly of light value. Despite the use of the very light bronze fabric and traces of black, the majority of fabrics in the quilt on page 30 are of medium value. In the quilt on page 29, with its liberal use of black, dark values dominate.

INTENSITY

The intensity or saturation of a color is its strength or purity. Bright colors are high in intensity; dull colors are low in intensity. When gray is added or when complementary colors—pairs of hues opposite each other on the color wheel—are mixed, the resulting color is muddy and very low in intensity. Look at the different gradations of color possible by mixing red and green. At one end of the scale is a bright, clear red of very high intensity. Gradually, the red becomes muted and is replaced by a muddy, low intensity color that contrasts sharply with the original bright red.

Within a quilt, intense colors stand out and command attention. The high-intensity red-violets and blue-greens of the quilt on page 30 vibrate with life, yet are saved from being too overpowering by the presence of lower-intensity fabrics in the same hues. The brilliant blue-green is used sparingly, kept in check by grayed versions in other bands. On page 31, strong hues, yet of grayed intensity, lend a sense of tranquillity to the quilt.

COLOR CONTRAST

Contrast is the perceived difference or variation between two colors. Understanding the elements of hue, value, and intensity is the secret to using contrast effectively, while maintaining overall unity. Let's look at some examples of Seminole bands to explain contrast and to see how its use makes different hues with different values and intensities work well together.

HIGH CONTRAST

High contrast is achieved by using two very different colors together. The sharpest contrast is between black and white, like the keys on a piano. The three bands here make different uses of contrast. The first shows a simple contrast of hue: yellow and violet offer the strongest light-dark contrast on the color wheel. The second shows contrast of value: a juxtaposition of light and dark fabrics. The last band shows contrast of intensity: a saturated red-violet stands out against the muddy, low-intensity green. Notice the crisp, hard edges in all three bands, a sign of high contrast.

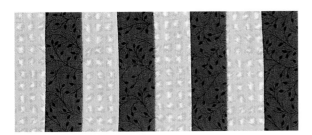

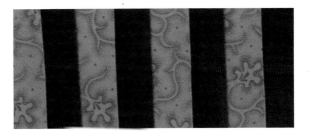

Compare our three sample quilts to see how areas of high contrast draw the eye. Notice how in the quilts on page 29 and page 30, light-dark pairings produce the highest degree of contrast, drawing you into each quilt. In the first quilt, it is not the vibrant fuchsia-black combination that forms the strongest contrast, but the lighter gold-black pairing. Remember this when deciding color placement. In the other two quilts, can you identify areas of high contrast? Which parts of the quilt jump to life as you look at it? What does this tell you about the quilter's use of contrast?

MEDIUM CONTRAST

With medium contrast, the edges between the colors are still crisp, but the effect is less harsh. This effect is achieved by using the different elements of color either to unify and provide harmony, or to provide the contrast necessary for diversity and variety. The ability to manipulate the elements of hue, value and intensity paves the way for a sophisticated and subtle use of color within a quilt. Let's see how this works in the pairs of bands pictured on the next page. The first two bands demonstrate medium contrast of hue. In the top band, the similar hues of red-violet blend pleasantly, while contrast of value keeps the edges distinct. In the bottom band, hue is used for contrast. The very dissimilar hues of red-violet and green-blue provide that contrast. Yet similar value and intensity keep the effect in check.

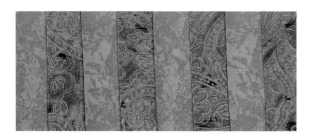

The next pair of bands demonstrates medium contrast of value. In the first, value is used to unify. The medium value of each fabric keeps these colors subdued. In the second band, value is used for contrast. The very similar brownish-orange hues are set apart by contrast of value—one light, the other mid-range dark.

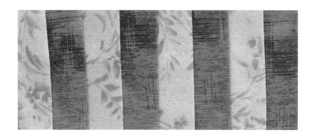

The last pair of bands demonstrates medium contrast of intensity. In the first band, intensity is used to unify. The striking pairing of yellow and violet works because of the very low intensity of each. In the second, intensity is used for contrast. The two yellow-orange fabrics are interesting because of the variations in intensity.

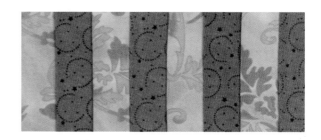

While areas of high contrast draw the eye into a quilt, it is bands of medium contrast that hold the viewer's attention. Looking again at the quilt on page 29, notice the repeating fuchsia-green pattern. Although the hues contrast, that contrast is muted by the similarity in value and intensity, subtly reinforcing the color message. Similarly, in the quilt on page 31, the white-blue Checkerboard pattern at the top of the quilt is of medium contrast, and the colors are repeated throughout the quilt.

LOW CONTRAST
Smooth gradation of color is achieved by positioning colors of low contrast together. The edges between the colors lose their definition so that the colors almost merge into one another. The following band uses hues that are next to each other on the color wheel, blue and bluegreen. There is almost no contrast of hue. Moreover, both are of similar value and intensity.

Next, complementary hues of similar light values—allow the eye to move gently through the band.

In the next band, the yellow and violet are drawn together through their grayed intensities.

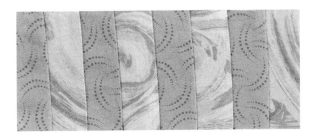

Within a quilt, while high contrast grabs the eye and medium contrast holds it, low contrast allows the eye to rest. The soft, textural effects of low contrast color use are best enjoyed up close. Barely noticeable from a distance, the light peach and gray-green fabric in the quilt on page 31 adds a certain delicacy to the quilt. Yet low contrast is not always as subtle. Look at the bright pink-bold gold combination in the quilt on page 29. Both high-intensity, warm colors, used in combination—the effect is dramatic.

As you begin creating Seminole bands, think of color in terms of hue, value, and intensity. It will help you exper-iment and you will find wonderful color combinations you may otherwise not have thought would work—or may not have dared to try. Understanding the elements of color helps us all explore new possibilities, with the result that our quilts become richer, more vibrant, more complex, more subtle—and more individual.

COLOR COMFORT

Even the most color confident among us have our favorite colors. These are the colors with which we are most at ease. Our closets are filled with them, our homes are decorated with them, and we even choose them when we make gifts for others. We feel comfort-able surrounded by colors we like and uneasy around those we don't. Awareness of our personal color com-fort zones can alert us to the fact that we may be miss-ing out on wonderful color opportunities by allowing ourselves to be guided by our own color preferences. Though it is perfectly acceptable to use colors we enjoy in a quilt, it is also good to keep an open mind about the merits of those that are less immediately appealing.

My personal color preference is for mid to dark values. Though I always admired quilts with a lavish use of lights, whenever I tried to use more lights, I became uncomfortable and usually retreated back into mid tones. On occasion, I persevered and forced myself to buy and work with light fabrics—always with surpris-ing results. I discovered that when light fabrics are slightly grayed in intensity, I find them a delight to use. Without this newfound knowledge, I would never have made a quilt such as the one on page 31, which I found extremely satisfying to make as well as enjoyable to own.

One of the attractions of Seminole piece work is that it is so easy to experiment with new or unusual colors.

The bands take so little time to make so that you can almost instantly see the results of your color choices. By exploring different colors, either as the key fabric in a quilt or as an accent fabric, you can expand your range of creative choices, adding depth and subtlety to your work.

ELEMENTS OF DESIGN

I like to think of design as purposeful visual creation. For me, a successful design is one that is both visually appealing and fulfills the expectations of its creator. Through its use of line, movement, and scale, a well-designed quilt both pleases and surprises. Yet there is no great mystery about design. There is no single principle that makes a quilt stand out, but, as we shall see, it is a combination of several different elements that give a quilt an overall effect of originality and excitement. As we explore the elements of design, we'll look at the three quilts pictured in this chapter to illustrate how each works.

SCALE

Scale refers to the relative size of the pieces that make up a design. A quilt composed of pieced units that are all the same size can seem monotonous, whereas carefully chosen variations in size add excitement. Making quilts through Seminole piecing allows many opportunities to experiment with scale, incorporating both large- and small-scale bands into the same quilt.

Compare the three sample quilts in this chapter to discover how important variation of scale is in avoiding monotony. Notice, for example, the variety of scale in the quilt on page 31. The bold Checkerboard and Arrowhead patterns are tempered by the finer lines of Maze/Letter T and Desert Flower. Some Seminole designs contain a variety of scale within the bands themselves. Look, for example, at Rattlesnake, Fraternal Peaks, and Medallion/Letter I.

POSITIVE AND NEGATIVE SPACE

Positive space appears to be occupied by an object, while negative space appears as background. However, as background often takes up much more space than the object within it, it must be selected with care. If a stronger color or fabric is chosen for the background than for the object or pattern, it can dominate the design. This effect—known as figure and ground reversal—can be interesting, but only if you are expecting it. To illustrate, the first example here is of two interlocking fabrics of equal weight or strength. Both take up equal amounts of space. Look what happens when one or the other is made the dominant fabric. This is just one of the effects possible when you experiment with positive and negative space.

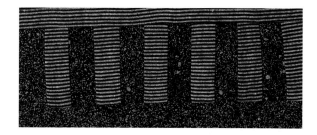

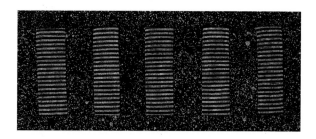

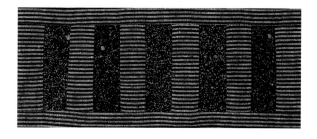

The quilts on pages 29 and 30 both use the Medallion/Letter I band. Notice how figure and ground reversal gives each an entirely different appearance.

LINE

The movement of a design is the path the eye takes as it looks at a quilt. Ideally, the eye will first be drawn to the focal point and then move through the quilt, with interesting pauses along the way. Use of lines, particularly in Seminole bands, plays an important part in controlling movement. Diagonal lines, for example, suggest action, drawing the eye through the pattern. Vertical and horizontal lines are more static, suggesting calm. In some bands, vertical lines forming figures move the eye step by step across the bands in a staccato movement, unlike the sweep of a diagonal. Varying the use of line goes a long way to adding life to a quilt.

Lines may also vary in scale—some wide, some narrow, some short, some long. Further, variety of line may be achieved by varying the width of the strips used as horizontal borders.

Analyze the diverse use of line in the quilt on page 30. Here, the light, narrow line of Fraternal Peaks captures the eye, drawing it across the quilt in an irregular pattern. The downward slope at the right border flings the eye down, drawn back into the quilt by the light horizontal bar. In the same quilt, contrast this frenetic

movement to the slow, inward turning of Snail Trail. Use of line in the quilt on page 31 is entirely different. Here, movement is steady and regular, perfectly suited to the formality of the fabric.

RHYTHM AND REPETITION

Several types of repetition are possible in Seminole that add rhythm to a design. The figure along a band, the color, or the width of the border can all repeat at intervals. Repetition gives a feeling of unity; the eye quickly learns to look for a pattern and repetition fulfills that expectation. Rhythm is determined by the interval between repetitions. Even spacing of a figure within a band creates a regular rhythm.

Irregular spacing is less predictable. Here, the grayed fabric blends with the low-value darks on either side of it, producing an irregular rhythm that sweeps the eye across the band.

The quilt on page 31 is restrained in its use of rhythm. Though steady and regular across individual bands, the pace quickens or slows with each. The rat-a-tat of the points of Crystals is rapid; the pace of Maze/Letter T is more studied. Checkerboard has a slow beat, and the light peach and red-orange of Synchopated Piano Keys give it a slow but steady rhythm. Contrast this with the staccato rhythm of the same band in the quilt on page 29. What else do you notice about the rhythm of the different bands in this quilt?

CHOOSING FABRICS FOR SEMINOLE QUILTS

Seminole is distinctive because of the exciting combinations of fabrics and colors possible, both in single bands and in an entire quilt. If you are like most quilters, it is the fabric that inspires you to start a new project. You see a fabric you can't resist—a rich floral, bright geometrical shapes, or a subtle bird or animal print. The fabric sets a mood, suggests a design, and creates an impression of colors working together. The quilt comes to life in your mind.

But wait. Before you head to the cutting table, take a good look at that special fabric. Unroll a yard or so from the bolt and spread it out, preferably in natural light. Open it out, selvage to selvage. Look for the repeat in the pattern. Make sure that if the repeat forms a stripe or a diagonal pattern, it is one you like. Check that there is no secondary or background pattern that makes the fabric difficult to work with. If you still like the fabric and plan to star it in your Seminole quilt, buy 1 to 1-½ yards (0.9 m to 1.4 m).

CHOOSING HARMONIOUS FABRICS

HUE
One you've bought the fabric that inspired you to make a quilt, analyze it in terms of the hues that are present and the hues you want to emphasize. If you decide on red-violets or blue-greens, for example, look for harmonious fabrics in those groups. Choose six or eight fabrics, then step back and evaluate them. Ask yourself:

- Does the selection support my original decision? If not, do I want to change color direction?
- Is there enough variation among the fabrics that patterns will be clearly defined? (High contrast)
- Will I be able to repeat the color message in several ways, without the quilt becoming harsh or jarring? (Medium contrast)
- Are there fabrics that will blend smoothly, adding subtlety? (Low contrast)

Think, also, in terms of some of the specific bands you plan on making. If you've chosen Rattlesnake, is there a fabric strong enough for the X pattern? Are there enough choices for the boxes? What about the background? Will the X pattern stand out or blend in?

VALUE
Evaluate your fabric selections in terms of light and dark. Is any fabric so light that it jumps out at you? Is this an effect you want? If not, consider adding slightly darker fabrics to create a gradual transition from light to dark. In general terms, what is the value range you'd like to achieve? Light to dark, mid to light, or mid to dark? Do you have a comfortable range, or would the quilt benefit from adding either lighter or darker fabrics for greater contrast, or from adding mid-range values for smoother transitions or gradations?

INTENSITY
It is easy to check for high-intensity fabrics, as they have a way of drawing the eye. Do you have enough to provide the spark you need? Do you have so many that they overwhelm the more subdued fabrics?

It is more difficult to check for low-intensity fabrics. Rearrange your selections, particularly the brighter ones. Do the combinations glow or is the effect flat? If it is flat, seek out some grayed fabrics. Though not particularly attractive by themselves, duller grays and browns have a way of making more exciting fabrics shine even more brightly.

DECIDING HOW MUCH FABRIC TO BUY

There is an important difference in buying fabrics for traditional block quilts and buying fabrics for Seminole. For block quilts you can buy in quarter-yard pieces or even fat quarters, making it affordable to experiment with a very broad range. This efficiency is not possible with Seminole, where a single band may require an entire quarter-yard of fabric, with none left over to repeat in other parts of the quilt.

The quilts in *Simply Seminole* measure approximately 45" x 70" (114 cm x 178 cm). Each requires a total of 7¼ yards (6.7 meters) of fabric, of which 2¾ yards (2.5 meters) is used for the backing. In making your selections for the remaining 4½ yards (4.2 meters), buy:

- Main fabric—1 to 1½ yards (0.9 to 1.4 meters)
- Harmonious hues—1½ to 2½ yards (1.4 to 2.3 meters) in quarter- and half-yard (meter) pieces
- Contrast value/intensity—1 to 1½ yards (0.9 to 1.4 meters) in quarter- and half-yard (meter) pieces

WORKING WITH COLORS AND FABRICS

Even on a limited budget, there are easy ways to collect a selection of fabric in a wide range of colors, enough for experimenting. Check out the back pages of quilting magazines. Often you may find offers such as "100 squares for $10.00." Perhaps these are not large enough pieces for making a quilt, but they are certainly large enough for color play. Friends may be willing to share their scraps as may other students in quilting classes. Collecting an assortment is key, it really doesn't matter how small the pieces are.

The exercises that follow will help take you through the process of selecting colors for use in making Seminole bands. The objective is to develop a personal color sense as you discover how to make the most of the colors you enjoy and how to expand upon that range. For each exercise, make sure you are working in natural light so that you see each color as it really is.

EXERCISE 1: ANALYZING COLORS

Choose a color of which you feel you have several samples. Let's suppose that you've chosen blue. Take out all the swatches containing blues from your collection and lay them on a large table or on the floor. Study each sample, comparing and contrasting them.

Next, arrange the swatches into a continuum, with as little contrast as possible between each swatch. This is harder to do than it sounds, and forces you to think in terms of color value and intensity. Set aside any blues you have that don't seem to fit and try them again once your continuum is complete. How smooth is the gradation? Are there any steps missing? Do you have both light and dark values? Both low and high intensities? What does this tell you about your color preferences? Revisit the fabric store and seek out samples of the missing colors. Fit them into the continuum. Do they improve the look of the band? Sometimes, it is those "missing" colors that will really hold a quilt together or add a feeling of excitement.

Are there any blues that you can't seem to fit into the continuum? Are they really blue at all? What does this tell you about your perception of color and your preferences? Do these misfits seem out of place on the continuum or do they add a certain sparkle?

Stand back and look at the entire grouping. Which sections of it do you like best? Which sections seem unexciting? Why do you think this is?

Form your swatches into a simple band like Piano Keys and keep this at hand whenever you are working with the color you chose. You can do the same for other colors you like or tend to use a lot in your quilts. As you begin planning a new quilt, you will be working with the broadest possible spectrum, not just with your favorite colors or with the ones in your fabric collection. Before you make final color decisions, the continuum helps you evaluate colors based on how well they work together.

EXERCISE 2: VALUE

Value changes as black or white is added to a color, producing tints (light) and shades (dark). In this exercise, you'll make a value continuum going from light to dark, with the selected color at the center.

Choose a color—either one that you like or of which you have several different samples. At one end of a long strip of card place a swatch of white. At the other end, place a swatch of black. Next, evaluate each swatch of your chosen color. Hold them against the black and white swatches, deciding exactly how light or dark each one is. Arrange them on the continuum according to light and dark. You'll find that the purest sample of your chosen color naturally falls in the center.

This exercise forces you to look closely at fabrics to determine exactly what the color is. If you are working with reds, for example, you may find that colors you thought of as pinks are actually red-orange or red-violet and do not fit well into the continuum. Or you may begin to see real differences among colors you had thought were the same—your collection of teals, for example, might break down into blue-greens or green-blues. Only once you analyze them can you see that they are not the same color at all and don't work well together.

Making distinctions, however small, between color values will bring greater subtlety to the quilts you create. You will be able to work with lights and darks so that your quilt, though made from pieces of the same basic color, gives an impression of variety and movement.

EXERCISE 3: INTENSITY

The intensity of a color is its strength or brightness. In this exercise, you'll create a continuum that will show you how color intensity can transform the look of a quilt.

Choose a color and select the brightest swatch you have, along with the muddiest or most grayed sample. Place these at either end of a long strip of card. See how many swatches you can find to fit in between them. Try to transition smoothly from one to the next. When you have analyzed each sample in your collection, take the strip to the fabric store. Try out new samples and decide how intense the color is in each.

Select a pair of complementary hues, such as red-green, blue-orange, or yellow-violet. Choose the clearest, most saturated samples you can find of each and place them at either end of a long strip of card. Select grayed versions of each of your two colors and position them on the strip to form a progression from one color to the other. As you reach the middle, notice how many browns or grays you have. Mix and match these low-intensity versions with the higher intensity colors at each end of the strip. See how brightly these high-intensity swatches stand out against the browns and grays.

EXERCISE 4: RHYTHM

Using the Piano Keys pattern (page 48), create a two-color band with a regular rhythm. Select two additional colors. Maintain the 1-2-1-2 rhythm using these colors. Now select colors for a 1-a-2-a rhythm. How many patterns can you create with four fabrics?

EXERCISE 5: FABRIC SELECTION

Either from your fabric collection or at the fabric store, choose a fabric that inspires you to start on a quilt. Hold it against other fabrics and select eight or ten samples, varying hue, intensity, and value, that you feel will work well with your first choice. Set the samples aside and begin again, this time seeking out eight or ten samples you feel are as different as possible from the first set, yet still complement the main fabric choice. If your first samples were dark, choose lights. If they were bright, choose grayed colors. Compare the two sets of samples. Are there some in the second set that appeal to you? Will they work as well or better than the samples you chose first?

THE CATALOG OF SEMINOLE DESIGNS

The bands are grouped by type: alternate, stairstep, floating, and angle. This grouping makes it easy to see the similarities between bands and so makes them simpler to make.

Though you can make each band in any size you wish, the directions are based on a finished width of 40" to 43" (102 cm to 110 cm). This is the selvage-to-selvage width of most commercial fabrics. All seam allowances are ¼" (0.6 cm).

If you run into difficulties making any of the bands, remember to turn back to the Ready Reference in Chapter 2 for help.

Chapter 4

ALTERNATE BANDS

45" x 72" (114 cm x 183 cm)
Betsy Robins, Port Angeles, WA
From top: Harlequin (stairstep); Piano Keys (alternate);
Telephone Poles variation (alternate); Piano Keys
variation (alternate); Peaks (angle).

CHECKERBOARD

Checkerboard is the simplest of Seminole designs. Made up of alternate squares in just two fabrics, it is more effectively used as an accent than as the focal point of a quilt. Once sewn into a quilt, the band measures 40½" x 4½" (102.9 cm x 11.4 cm).

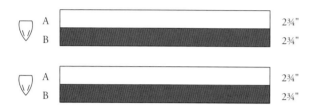

Cut and Stitch

STRIP SET. Cut two 2¾" (7 cm) strips each of fabrics A and B, each measuring at least 28" (71.1 cm). Stitch two sets together lengthwise.

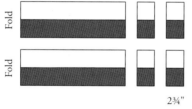

Fold and Slice

SEGMENTS. Fold in half end to end and slice into 2-¾" (7 cm) segments.

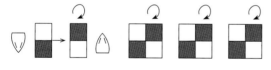

Flip and Stitch

SECTIONS. Flip every second segment upside down and stitch together in pairs to create sections, matching the center seams.

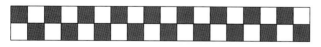

Join Band

BAND. Stitch the sections edge to edge to complete the Checkerboard band.

As a variation, try cutting the strips into segments of 4" (10.2 cm) instead of 2½" (6.4 cm). This simple change gives Checkerboard an altogether different look.

FLIP FLOP

The name of this band says it all. Simple to create yet making a strong impact, these alternate large and small rectangles allow multiple fabric choices and a lively contrast of scale. Once sewn into a quilt, the band measures 45" x 9" (114.3 cm x 22.9 cm).

STRIP SET. Cut four strips of fabric, selvage to selvage, as follows:

> One 3¾" (9.5 cm) strip of Fabric A
>
> One 1¾" (6.4 cm) strip of Fabric B
>
> One 1¾" (4.4 cm) strip of Fabric C
>
> One 3¾" (9.5 cm) strip of Fabric D

Cut one more strip of each, measuring at least 12" (30 cm), in the same widths. Stitch together lengthwise as shown.

Cut and Stitch

SEGMENTS. Fold in half end to end and slice into 2¾" (7 cm) segments.

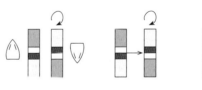

Fold and Slice

SECTIONS. Stitch the segments edge to edge, matching seamlines and flipping alternate segments.

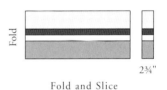

Flip and Stitch

BAND. Stitch the sections edge to edge to complete the Flip Flop band.

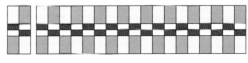

Join Band

PIANO KEYS

It is easy to picture the Piano Keys pattern—simple vertical rectangles that alternate between two fabrics. If you wish, you can use more than two fabrics, repeating the pattern across the band. Once sewn into a quilt, the band measures 42" x 2½" (106.7 cm x 6.4 cm).

Cut and Stitch

STRIP SET. Cut two 1¼" (3.2 cm) strips each of fabrics A and B, selvage to selvage. Stitch together lengthwise, alternating fabrics.

Fold and Slice

SEGMENT. Fold in half end to end and slice into 3" (7.6 cm) segments.

Stitch

SECTIONS. Stitch the segments edge to edge, alternating fabrics.

Join Band

BAND. Stitch the sections edge to edge to complete the Piano Keys band.

Try making the band at half height—1½" (3.8 cm), perhaps for one of the borders of your quilt. It can nicely accent the colors used in more dramatic bands.

48

SYNCOPATED PIANO KEYS

This is a slightly more intricate variation on Piano Keys. The alternating pattern is the same, but by varying the width of segments, the band takes on a less regular rhythm. It can be made in two or more fabric choices. Once sewn into a quilt, the band measures 42" x 3½" (106.7 cm x 8.9 cm).

STRIP SET. Cut four strips of fabric, selvage to selvage, as follows, plus an additional 14" (35.6 cm) strip of each:

> One 1⅛" (2.8 cm) strip of Fabric A
>
> One 1⅜" (3.5 cm) strip of Fabric B
>
> One ¾" (1.9 cm) strip of extra Fabric A
>
> One ⅞" (2.2 cm) strip of Fabric B

You can use two or four different fabrics, but maintain a light/dark pattern. Stitch together lengthwise as shown.

Cut and Stitch

SEGMENTS. Fold in half end to end and slice into 3" (7.6 cm) segments.

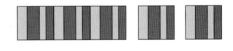

Fold and Slice

SECTIONS. Stitch the segments edge to edge, alternating fabrics.

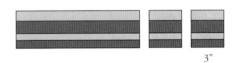

Stitch

BAND. Stitch the sections edge to edge to complete the Syncopated Piano Keys band.

Join Band

TELEPHONE POLES

Telephone Poles looks as it name suggests–strong verticals with double crossbars. A bold, large-scale pattern, it usually has a strong presence in a quilt. Telephone Poles is easy to make using just two fabrics. Once sewn into a quilt, the band measures 45¼" x 7¾" (114.9 cm x 19.7 cm).

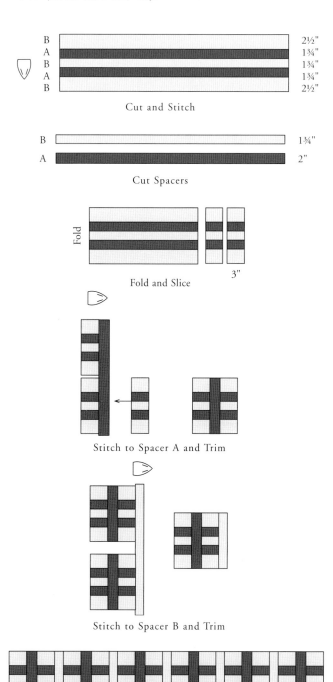

Cut and Stitch

Cut Spacers

Fold and Slice

Stitch to Spacer A and Trim

Stitch to Spacer B and Trim

Join Band

STRIP SET. Cut five strips of fabric selvage to selvage as follows:

> Two 1¾" (4.4 cm) strips of Fabric A
> Two 2½" (6.4 cm) strips of Fabric B
> One 1¾" (4.4 cm) strips of Fabric B

For use as spacers, cut two strips selvage to selvage as follows, plus an additional 8½" (21.6 cm) strip of each:

> One 2" (5.1 cm) strip of Fabric A
> One 1¾" (4.4 cm) strip of Fabric B

Stitch the strips together lengthwise as shown. Set aside the extra spacer strips.

SEGMENTS. Fold in half end to end and slice the strip set into 3" (7.6 cm) segments.

SECTIONS. One at a time, stitch half the segments to the 2" (5.1 cm) spacer strip of Fabric A. Trim strip even with raw edges of segment. Next, stitch the remaining segments to the opposite edge of the strip. Match the seams across this center strip.

Repeat, this time stitching the partial sections onto either side of the 1¾" (4.4 cm) spacer strip of Fabric B.

BAND. Stitch the sections edge to edge to complete the Telephone Poles band.

A beautiful variation is to use a mix of background fabrics, gradating background colors across the band so that it looks like poles against the sunrise.

L E T T E R   H

Letter H is easy to make in two fabrics. With its steady rhythm and large scale, it provides a stabilizing influence within a quilt. Once sewn into a quilt, the band measures 40" x 6" (101.6 cm x 15.2 cm).

STRIP SETS. Cut six strips of fabric, selvage to selvage, as follows:

> Two 2" (5.1 cm) strips of Fabric A
>
> Two 3" (7.6 cm) strips of Fabric B
>
> One 2½" (6.4 cm) strip of Fabric A
>
> One 2½" (6.4 cm) strip of Fabric B

Stitch together lengthwise as shown to form two strip sets.

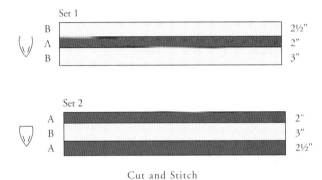

Cut and Stitch

SEGMENTS. Fold Set 1 in half end to end and slice into 2½" (6.4 cm) segments.

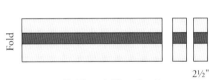

Fold and Slice Set 1

SECTIONS. One at a time, stitch the segments to Set 2. Slice through Set 2 after the segments are attached to trim even with the raw edges of the segments.

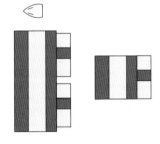

Stitch to Set 2 and Trim

BAND. Stitch the sections edge to edge to complete the Letter H band.

Join Band

SNAIL TRAIL

This band imitates in straight lines the circular pattern a snail might leave in its wake. Though it uses just two fabrics, Snail Trail really stands out, particularly when made in high-contrast colors. Snail Trail requires special attention to get the left/right placement exact and to achieve crisp seam matches. Once sewn into a quilt, the band measures 42" x 7" (106.7 cm x 17.8 cm).

A   1½"
B   1½"

Cut and Stitch

A   1½"
B   1½"

Cut Spacers

STRIP SETS. Cut ten strips of fabric, selvage to selvage, as follows:

> Five 1½" (3.8 cm) strips of Fabric A
>
> Five 1½" (3.8 cm) strips of Fabric B

Stitch together lengthwise as shown to form three identical strip sets. Set aside the extra strips.

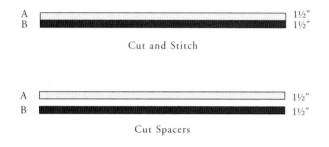

1½"   2½"   4½"

Fold and Slice

SEGMENTS. Fold in half end to end and slice into segments. Make seven 1½" (3.8 cm) segments; fourteen 2½" (6.4 cm) segments; and fourteen 4½" (11.4 cm) segments.

Stitch Section 1   Stitch Section 2   Stitch Section 3
and Trim   and Trim   and Trim

SECTIONS. Stitch two 2½" (6.4 cm) segments to each 1½" (3.8 cm) segment in the order shown to create Section 1. Stitch seven 4½" (11.4cm) segments to one of the spacer strips of Fabric A to create Section 2. Stitch the remaining seven 4½" (11.4 cm) segments to one of the spacer strips of Fabric B to create Section 3.

3   1   2

Stitch Sections

BAND. Stitch Sections 1, 2, and 3 together in the order shown, matching seamlines. Stitch the sections edge to edge to form a band. Stitch the remaining strips of Fabrics A and B to either side of the band, as shown.

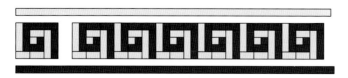

Join Band and Add Band Edges

C R O S S

This simple cross shape is as easy to make as it looks. Very effective in three fabrics, ? ??? ???? ??? ??? ??? ?????????, ??? ??? ???
cross itself, and one for the center square. This band forms the center section of Tumbling Cross (page 68). Once sewn into a
quilt, the band measures 41½" x 6" (105.4 cm x 15.2 cm).

STRIP SETS. Cut three strips of fabric, each measuring at least 30" (76.2 cm), as follows:

> One 2" (5.1 cm) strip of Fabric A
>
> Two 2½" (6.4 cm) strips of Fabric B

Cut three more strips of fabric, each measuring at least 14" (35.6 cm), as follows:

> Two 2½" (6.4 cm) strips of Fabric A
>
> One 2" (5.1 cm) strip of Fabric C

For use as a spacer, cut an additional 2" (5.1 cm) strip of Fabric B, selvage to selvage. Stitch the strips together lengthwise as shown to form two strip sets. Set the spacer strip aside.

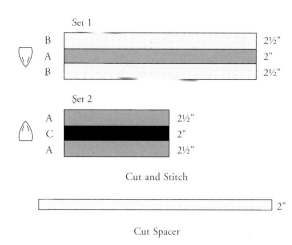

SEGMENTS. Fold both sets in half, end to end. Slice Set 1 into 2½" (6.4 cm) segments. Slice Set 2 into 2" (5.1 cm) segments.

SECTIONS. Stitch together alternating segments in a Set 1–Set 2–Set 1 pattern, matching seamlines. Stitch to the 2" (5.1 cm) spacer strip of Fabric B as shown. Trim.

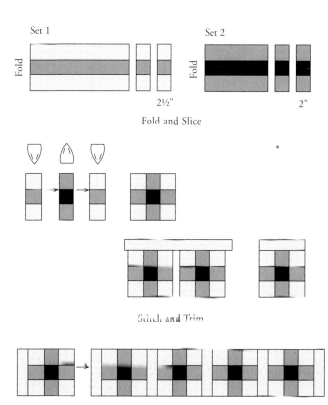

BAND. Stitch the sections edge to edge to complete the Cross band.

MEDALLION/LETTER I

Depending on color placement, this band looks like two different things: a medallion with a center rectangle or a capital letter I. This dual image makes the band an excellent one for experimenting with figure and ground reversal (see page 36). Made from three fabrics and constructed from two strip sets, the band is nevertheless easy to piece. Once sewn into a quilt, the band measures 42" x 5" (106.7 cm x 12.7 cm).

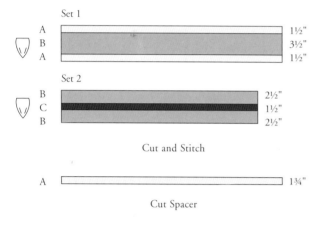

Cut and Stitch

Cut Spacer

STRIP SETS. Cut three strips of fabric, each measuring at least 30" (76.2 cm), as follows:

> Two 1½" (3.8 cm) strips of Fabric A
>
> One 3½" (8.9 cm) strip of Fabric B

Cut three more strips of fabric, each measuring at least 18" (45.7 cm), as follows:

> Two 2½" (6.4 cm) strips of Fabric B
>
> One 1½" (3.8 cm) strip of Fabric C

For use as a spacer, cut an additional 1¾" (4.4 cm) strip of Fabric A, selvage to selvage. Stitch the strips together lengthwise as shown to form two strip sets. Set the spacer strip aside.

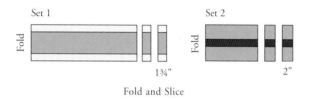

Fold and Slice

SEGMENTS. Fold both sets in half, end to end. Slice Set 1 into sixteen 1¾" (4.4 cm) segments. Slice Set 2 into eight 2" (5.1 cm) segments.

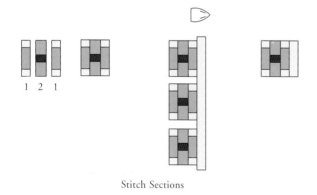

Stitch Sections

SECTIONS. Stitch together alternating segments in a Set 1–Set 2–Set 1 pattern, matching seamlines. Stitch to the 1¾" (4.4 cm) spacer strip of Fabric A as shown. Trim.

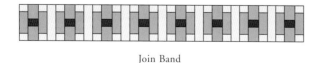

Join Band

BAND. Stitch the sections edge to edge to complete the Medallion band.

MAZE / LETTER T

Maze is the most intricate of alternate designs, yet is surprisingly simple to make. The use of narrow strips makes this small-scale pattern subtle and understated, a delicate contrast to bolder bands. It uses three fabrics. Once sewn into a quilt, the band measures 41¼" x 6¼" (104.8 cm x 15.9 cm).

STRIP SETS. Cut nine strips of fabric, each measuring at least 28" (71.1 cm), as follows:

> Two 1¼" (3.2 cm) strips of Fabric A
>
> Two 1¼" (3.2 cm) strips of Fabric B
>
> Four 1½" (3.8 cm) strips of Fabric B
>
> Two 1¼" (3.2 cm) strips of Fabric C

For use as spacers, cut a 1½" (3.8 cm) strip each of Fabric A and Fabric C, selvage to selvage. Stitch the strips together lengthwise as shown to form four strip sets. Press seams toward darker fabric. Set the spacer strips aside.

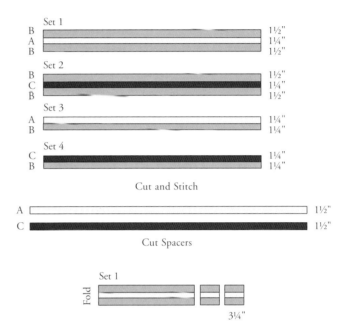

Cut and Stitch

Cut Spacers

SEGMENTS. Fold Set 1 and Set 2 in half, end to end. Slice both into 3¼" (8.3 cm) segments.

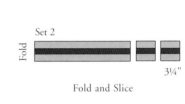

Fold and Slice

SECTIONS. Stitch segments made from Set 1 to Set 3. Stitch segments made from Set 2 to Set 4. Trim. Flip all sections made from Sets 2 and 4.

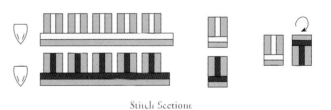

Stitch Sections

BAND. Stitch the sections edge to edge, alternating flipped and upright sections. To complete the Letter T band, stitch the 1½" (3.8 cm) spacer strips of Fabrics A and C to either edge.

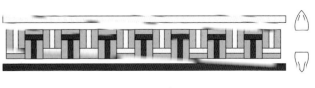

Join Band

Chapter 5

STAIRSTEP BANDS

45" x 72" (114 cm x 183 cm)
From top: Criss Cross variation (stairstep);
Rick Rack (stairstep); Harlequin (stairstep);
Box Kites (stairstep); Dominoes (stairstep);
Interlock (stairstep).

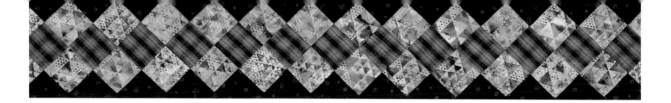

H A R L E Q U I N

Harlequin is made up of a line of interlocking squares placed on the diagonal. You may use up to five fabrics, allowing enormous variety within the same band. Here, we use three fabrics. Once sewn into a quilt, the band measures 45" x 7" (114.3 cm x 17.8 cm).

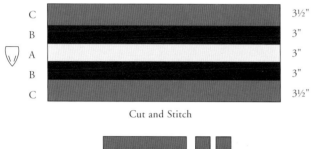

Cut and Stitch

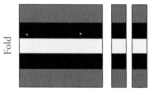

Fold and Slice   3"

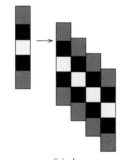

Stitch

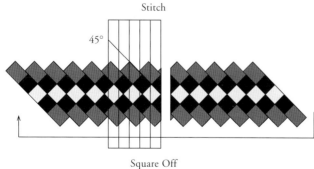

Square Off

STRIP SET. Cut five strips of fabric, selvage to selvage, as follows:

> One 3" (7.6 cm) strip of Fabric A
> Two 3" (7.6 cm) strips of Fabric B
> Two 3½" (8.9 cm) strips of Fabric C

Stitch together lengthwise as shown.

SEGMENTS. Fold the strip set in half end to end and slice into 3" (7.6 cm) segments.

SECTIONS. Stitch the segments together in a stairstep pattern as shown, matching seamlines to create section. Seams should interlock.

BAND. Square off the ends of the section by slicing through the section once and transferring the slice to the opposite end. Both ends will now be square. Trim the edges to form the Harlequin band.

Harlequin is a wonderful band for experimenting with colors. See how different it looks when symmetrical, gradated, or random colors are used. Add up to two more 3" (7.6 cm) strips per variation. Make sure the 3½" (8.9 cm) strips remain on the outside edges.

Trim

R I C K - R A C K

Typically using four fabrics or colors, Rick-Rack is made up of double sets of triangles or offset triangles. Easy to make, the triangles can be matched together in several ways for an entirely different look. Once sewn into a quilt the band measures 42" x 4½" (106.7 cm x 11.4 cm).

STRIP SETS. Cut four strips of fabric, selvage to selvage, as follows:

> One 3¾" (9.5 cm) strip of Fabric A
>
> One 3¾" (9.5 cm) strip of Fabric B
>
> One 3¾" (9.5 cm) strip of Fabric C
>
> One 3¾" (9.5 cm) strip of Fabric D

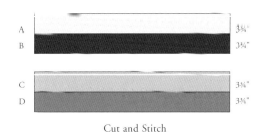

Cut and Stitch

Stitch together lengthwise as shown to form two strip sets. On the back of each set, make a chalk line 3" (7.6 cm) from the seamline.

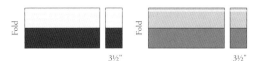

Fold and Slice

SEGMENTS. Fold both sets in half, end to end, and slice into 3½" (8.9 cm) segments.

SECTIONS. Within each set, stitch the segments edge to edge, matching the seamlines to the chalk lines.

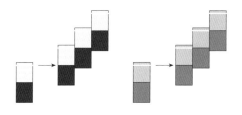

Stitch

BAND. To square off the ends, slice through each section once and transfer the slice to the opposite end, matching the chalk line to the seamline. Both ends will now be square. To complete the band, trim and match the two sections or use separately.

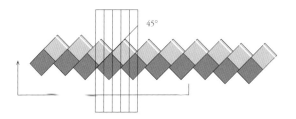

Square Off

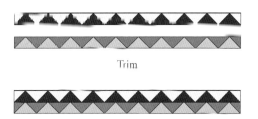

Trim

Match Sections

I N T E R L O C K

Depending on colors, Interlock can be a very dynamic pattern, setting off the entire quilt. Narrow rectangles interlock on the diagonal and undulate across the band. Though the band is not difficult to make, it is very important to take care with left/right placement. Once sewn into a quilt, the band measures 40" x 7½"(101.6 cm x 19.1 cm).

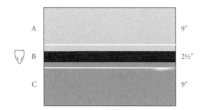

Cut and Stitch

STRIP SET. Cut three strips of fabric, each measuring at least 28" (71.1 cm), as follows:

> One 9" (22.9 cm) strip of Fabric A
>
> One 2½" (6.4 cm) strip of Fabric B
>
> One 9" (22.9cm) strip of Fabric C

Stitch together lengthwise as shown. On the back of the fabric, mark a chalk line 1¼" (3.2 cm) from each seamline.

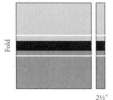

Fold and Slice

SEGMENTS. Fold in half, end to end, and slice into 2½" (6.4 cm) segments.

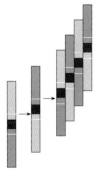

Stitch

SECTIONS. Flip alternate segments and stitch together, matching the chalk line to the seamline.

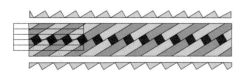

Trim

BAND. Trim the edges parallel with the top corner of the center squares. To square off the ends, slice through the section once and transfer the slice to the opposite end, matching the chalk line to the seamline. Both ends will now be square.

CRISS-CROSS

In this striking band, crosses seem almost to float on a background fabric, appearing at regular intervals. Though it is not difficult to make, assembling the band takes care. Once sewn into a quilt, the band measures 12" x 7" (22.1 cm x 17.8 cm).

STRIP SETS. Cut five strips of fabric, measuring at least 18" (45.7 cm) as follows:

> One 3¼" (8.2 cm) strip of Fabric A
> One 2½" (6.4 cm) strip of Fabric B
> One 2½" (6.4 cm) strip of Fabric D
> One 3" (7.6 cm) strip of Fabric C
> One 3¼" (8.2 cm) strip of Fabric A

Cut three strips of fabric, measuring at least 22" (55.9 cm), as follows:

> One 3¼" (8.3 cm) strip of Fabric A
> One 2½" (6.4 cm) strip of Fabric C
> One 7½" (20.3 cm) strip of Fabric A

Stitch together lengthwise as shown to form two strip sets. On the back of the 7¼" (18.4 cm) strip of Fabric A, mark a chalk line 5" (12.7 cm) from the seamline.

SEGMENTS. Slice Set 1 into six 2½" (6.4cm) segments. Slice Set 2 into six 3" (7.6 cm) segments.

SECTIONS. Take two segments from each set. Flip one from each set. Sew these four segments together in the order shown to create a section. Repeat twice. You now have three sections.

BAND. To join the sections, match the chalk lines to the seamlines and stitch. To square off the ends, slice through the section equidistant between crosses once and transfer the slice to the opposite end, matching the chalk line to the seamline. Both ends will now be square. Trim.

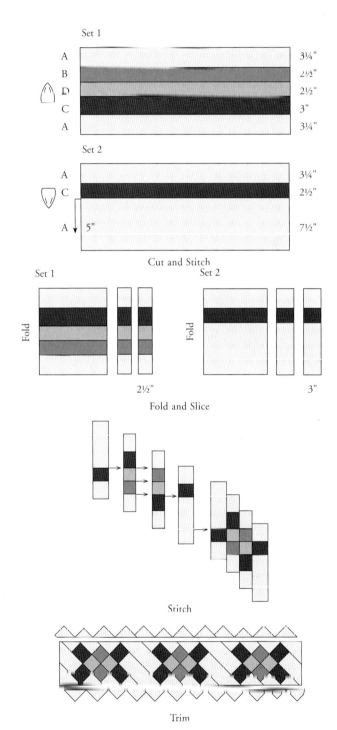

61

D O M I N O E S

Even and steady, the tiny rectangles that make up this pattern topple across the band. Because of the mix of colors possible, Dominoes is a wonderful opportunity to pick up and repeat colors used in the bolder bands of a quilt. Once sewn into a quilt, the band measures 39" x 5½" (99 cm x 14 cm).

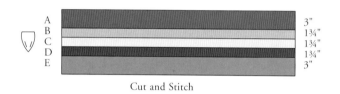

A   3"
B   1¾"
C   1¾"
D   1¾"
E   3"

Cut and Stitch

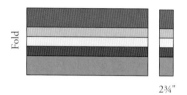

Fold

2¾"

Fold and Slice

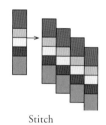

Stitch

STRIP SET. Cut five strips of fabric, selvage to selvage, as follows:

> One 3" (7.6 cm) strip of Fabric A
> One 1¾" (4.4 cm) strip of Fabric B
> One 1¾" (4.4 cm) strip of Fabric C
> One 1¾" (4.4 cm) strip of Fabric D
> One 3" (7.6 cm) strip of Fabric E

Stitch together lengthwise as shown.

SEGMENTS. Slice into 2¾" (7 cm) segments.

SECTIONS. Match and sew together in a stairstep pattern to create a section.

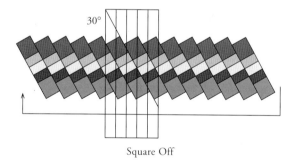

30°

Square Off

BAND. To square off the ends of the section, place a quilters' ruler's 30º mark on a seamline. Slice through the section once and transfer the slice to the opposite end. Both ends will now be square. Trim.

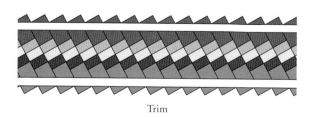

Trim

62

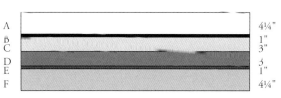

BOX KITES

With its chunky boxes and tiny accent strips, this band is the perfect choice to establish a color direction. Easy to make, it adds a lighthearted touch as the kites fly across the quilt. Once sewn into a quilt, the band measures 42" x 6½" (106.7 cm x 16.5 cm).

STRIP SET. Cut six strips of fabric, selvage to selvage, as follows:

> One 4¼" (10.8 cm) strip of Fabric A
>
> One 1" (2.5 cm) strip of Fabric B
>
> One 3" (7.6 cm) strip of Fabric C
>
> One 3" (7.6 cm) strip of Fabric D
>
> One 1" (2.5 cm) strip of Fabric E
>
> One 4¼" (10.8 cm) strip of Fabric F

Stitch together lengthwise as shown.

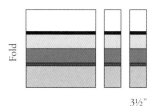

Cut and Stitch

SEGMENTS. Slice into 3½" (8.9 cm) segments.

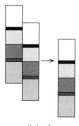

Fold and Slice

SECTIONS. Match and sew together in a stairstep pattern to create a section.

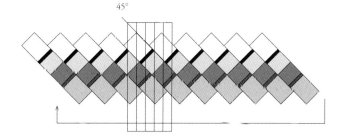

Stitch

BAND. To square off the ends of the section, place a quilters' ruler's 45° mark on a seamline. Slice through the section once and transfer the slice to the opposite end. Both ends will now be square. Trim.

Square Off

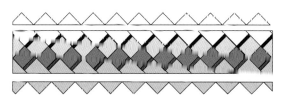

Trim

Chapter 6

FLOATING BANDS

45" x 72" (114 cm x 183 cm)
From top: Tumbling Glass (floating); Greek in the Embrace (floating);
Desert Flower (floating); Tumbling Josh (floating);
Weave (floating); Broken Chain (floating).

TUMBLING FISH

Tumbling Fish is the simplest of the floating-band designs. The squares are formed by strips of fabric, rotated so that they appear to be rolling. Though it uses four fabrics, Tumbling Fish is not particularly elaborate and makes a good support band for more complex designs. Once sewn into a quilt, the band measures 42" x 7" (106.7 cm x 17.8 cm).

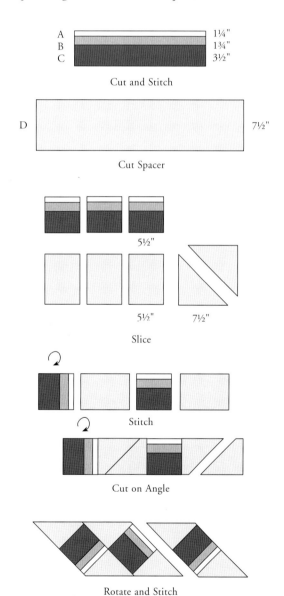

STRIP SET. Cut three strips of fabric, each measuring at least 33" (83.8 cm), as follows:

  One 1¼" (3.2 cm) strip of Fabric A

  One 1¾" (4.4 cm) strip of Fabric B

  One 3½" (8.9 cm) strip of Fabric C

For use as a spacer, cut one 7½" (19 cm) strip, selvage to selvage, of Fabric D. Stitch the strips together lengthwise as shown. Set aside the spacer strip.

SEGMENTS. Slice the set into five 5½" (14 cm) segments. Slice the spacer strip into five 5½" (14 cm) segments, plus one 7½" x 7½" (19 cm) square. Cut the square diagonally to make two triangles.

SECTIONS. Stitch the segments and alternating spacers edge to edge. Cut through the spacer at a 45° angle, equidistant between seamlines.

BAND. Rotate the sections and stitch edge to edge, matching seamlines. Use the two triangles to square the edges and form the Tumbling Fish band.

Square Off

R A T T L E S N A K E

In Rattlesnake, squares seem to cling to a floating X yet the band is transformed with the use of different spacer strips. Though the band is not difficult to make, matching the seams carefully makes all the difference. Large scale and eye catching, Rattlesnake can easily be the primary design in a Seminole quilt. Once sewn into a quilt, the band measures 44" x 9" (111.8 cm x 22.9 cm).

STRIP SET. Cut three strips of fabric, each measuring at least 30" (76.2 cm), as follows:

> One 2¾" (7 cm) strip of Fabric A
>
> One 1¼" (3.2 cm) strip of Fabric C
>
> One 2¾" (7 cm) strip of Fabric D

Cut two spacer strips of fabric, each measuring at least 30" (76.2 cm), as follows:

> One 7¾" (19.7 cm) strip of Fabric B
>
> One 1¼" (3.2 cm) strip of Fabric C

Stitch the strips together lengthwise as shown. Set aside the spacer strips.

SEGMENTS. Slice the set into ten 2¾" (7 cm) segments. Slice the 7¾" (19.7 cm) spacer strip into five 5¾" (14.6 cm) segments.

SECTIONS. Stitch half the segments to the 1¼" (3.2 cm) spacer strip as shown. Trim the strip even with the edges of the segment. Flip the remaining segments and stitch to the other side of the spacer strip, matching seams across the spacer strip.

BAND. Stitch the sections and alternating 5¾" (14.6 cm) spacers edge to edge. Cut through the spacer at a 45º angle, equidistant between seamlines. Rotate the sections and stitch edge to edge, matching seamlines. Square off the ends of the section by slicing through the section once and transferring the slice to the opposite end. Both ends will now be square forming the Rattlesnake band.

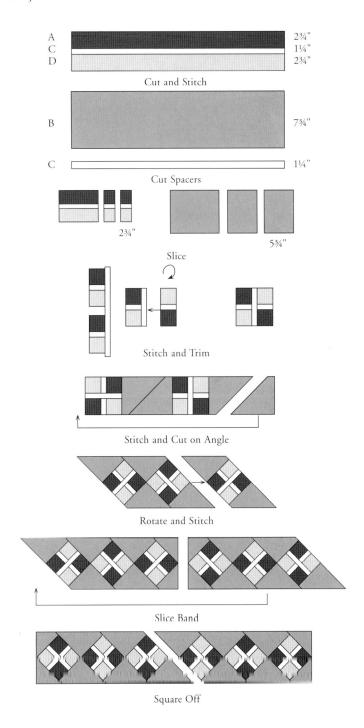

Cut and Stitch

Cut Spacers

Slice

Stitch and Trim

Stitch and Cut on Angle

Rotate and Stitch

Slice Band

Square Off

TUMBLING CROSS

Tumbling Cross is a terrific band to use when experimenting with different fabrics and colors. Easy to make, the look of the band is transformed when the colors are varied. Once sewn into a quilt, the band measures 45½" x 9½" (115.6 cm x 24.1 cm).

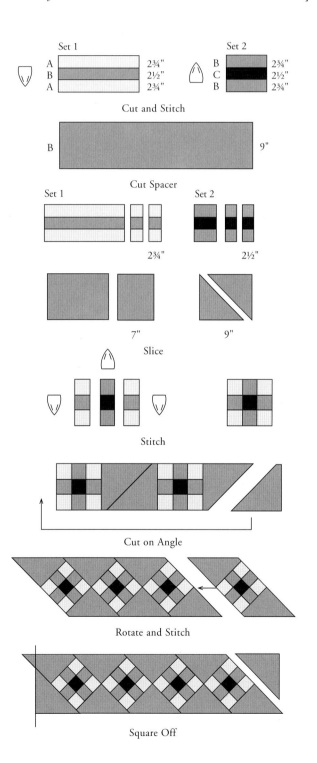

STRIP SETS. Cut three strips of fabric, each measuring at least 25" (63.5 cm), as follows:

> Two 2¾" (7 cm) strips of Fabric A
>
> One 2½" (6.4 cm) strip of Fabric B

Cut three strips of fabric, each measuring at least 13" (33 cm), as follows:

> Two 2¾" (7 cm) strips of Fabric B
>
> One 2½" (6.4 cm) strip of Fabric C

For use as a spacer, cut one 9" (22.9 cm) strip, selvage to selvage, of Fabric D. Stitch the strips together lengthwise into two sets as shown. Set the spacer strip aside.

SEGMENTS. Slice Set 1 into eight 2¾" (7 cm) segments. Slice Set 2 into four 2½"" (6.4 cm) segments. Slice the spacer into four 7" (17.8 cm) segments and one 9" x 9" square (22.9 cm). Slice the square diagonally to make two triangles.

SECTIONS. Stitch the segments edge to edge in the order shown to form sections.

BAND. Stitch the sections and alternating spacers edge to edge. Cut through the spacers at a 45° angle, equidistant between seamlines. Rotate the sections and stitch edge to edge, matching seamlines. Use the two triangles to square the edges and form the Tumbling Cross band. Trim.

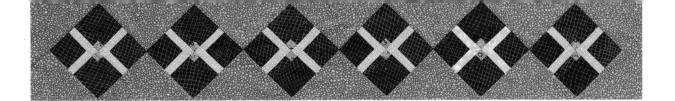

W E A V E

Delicate yet eye-catching, the lines in Weave seem to form knots which float in space. Though it's not difficult to make, this intricate design demands careful left/right placement and exact seamlines. Once sewn into a quilt, the band measures 44" x 6¼" (111.8 cm x 15.9 cm).

STRIP SETS. Cut three strips of fabric, each measuring at least 30" (76.2 cm), as follows:

> One 1" (2.5 cm) strip of Fabric A
> One 2¼" (5.7 cm) strip of Fabric B
> One 2¾" (7 cm) strip of Fabric B

Cut three strips of fabric, each measuring at least 13" (33 cm), as follows:

> One 2¾" (7 cm) strip of Fabric A
> One 2¼" (5.7 cm) strip of Fabric B
> One 1" (2.5 cm) strip of Fabric C

For use as a spacer, cut one 7" (83.8 cm) strip, selvage to selvage, of Fabric D. Stitch the strips together lengthwise as shown to form two strip sets. Set the spacer aside.

SEGMENTS. Slice Set 1 into twelve 2¼" (5.7 cm) segments. Slice Set 2 into twelve 1" (2.5 cm) segments. Slice the spacer into six 5" (12.7 cm) segments and one 7" x 7" (83.8 cm) square. Slice the square diagonally to make two triangles.

SECTIONS. Stitch the segments edge to edge in the order shown to form six: Set 1, Set 2, flipped Set 2, flipped Set 1.

BAND. Stitch the sections and alternating spacers edge to edge. Cut through the spacers at a 45° angle, equidistant between seamlines. Rotate and stitch edge to edge, matching seamlines. Use the two triangles to square the edges and form the Weave band.

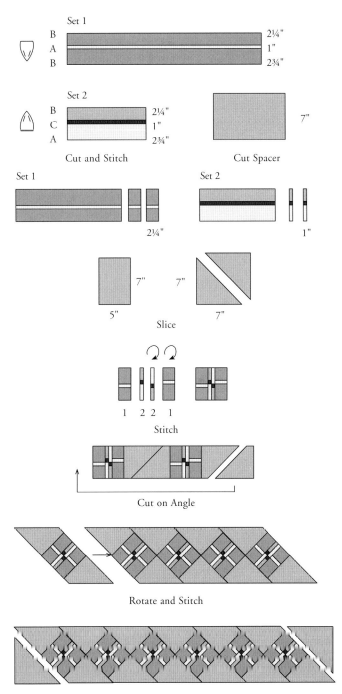

69

B R O K E N   C H A I N

Picture Broken Chain as a row of Cs falling into each other. The band is easy and effective to make in just two colors. Though simple, this large-scale design has impact and can be the primary pattern in a Seminole quilt. Once sewn into a quilt, the band measures 40" x 9" (101.6 cm x 22.9 cm).

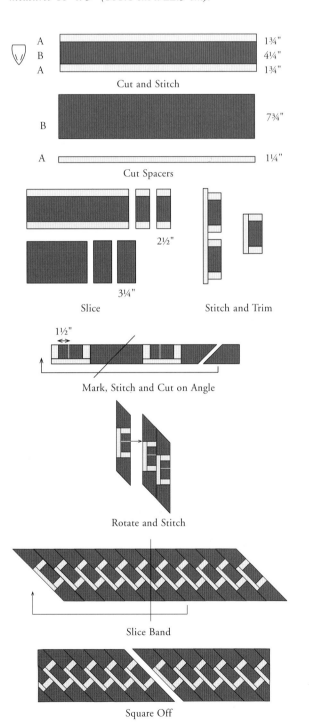

A
B
A

1¾"
4¼"
1¾"

Cut and Stitch

B

7¾"

A

1¼"

Cut Spacers

2½"

3¼"

Slice

Stitch and Trim

1½"

Mark, Stitch and Cut on Angle

Rotate and Stitch

Slice Band

Square Off

STRIP SET. Cut three strips of fabric, each measuring 27" (68.6 cm) as follows:

> Two 1¾" (4.4 cm) strips of Fabric A
> One 4¼" (10.8 cm) strip of Fabric B

For use as spacers, cut three strips, selvage to selvage.

> Two 1¼" (3.2 cm) strips of Fabric A
> One 7¾" (19.7 cm) strip of Fabric B

Stitch the strips together lengthwise as shown. Set the spacer strips aside.

SEGMENTS. Slice the set into eleven 2½" (6.4 cm) segments. Slice the 7¾" (19.7 cm) spacer into eleven 3¼" (8.3 cm) segments.

SECTIONS. Stitch the segments edge to edge to the 1¼" (3.8 cm) spacer strip as shown. Trim. Make a chalk mark 1½" (3.8 cm) from the lower left seamline of each section.

BAND. Stitch the sections and alternating spacers edge to edge. Cut through the spacers at a 45° angle, equidistant between seamlines. Rotate and stitch edge to edge, matching the chalk mark to the upper seamline. Square off the ends of the section by slicing through the section once and transferring the slice to the opposite end. Both ends will now be square, forming the Broken Chain band.

DESERT FLOWER

Zigzags make up the edges of Desert Flower, with flower-like criss-crosses springing up along the band. Not for beginners, this striking five fabric band requires careful attention to placement and wise color choices. Once sewn into a quilt, the band measures 40" x 8" (101.6 cm x 20.3 cm).

STRIP SETS. Cut three strips of fabric, each measuring at least 28" (71.1 cm), as follows:

> One 1¼" (3.2 cm) strip of Fabric A
>
> One 1¾" (4.4 cm) strip of Fabric B
>
> One 2¼" (5.7 cm) strip of Fabric B

Cut three strips, each at least 10" (25.4 cm):

> One 1¾" (4.4 cm) strip of Fabric A
>
> One 2¼" (5.7 cm) strip of Fabric A
>
> One 1¼" (3.2 cm) strip of Fabric C

For use as spacers, cut three strips, selvage to selvage:

> One 1¼" (3.2 cm) strip of Fabric B
>
> Two 1¼" (3.2 cm) strips of Fabric D

And cut two strips, each measuring 30" (76.2 cm):

> One 5" (12.7 cm) strip of Fabric B
>
> One 5" (12.7 cm) strip of Fabric E

Stitch together lengthwise to form two strip sets as shown.

SEGMENTS. Slice Set 1 into six 2¼" (5.7 cm) and six 1¾" (4.4 cm) segments; Set 2 into six 1¼" (3.2 cm) segments; and the two 5" (12.7 cm) spacers into three 8" (20.3 cm) segments.

SECTIONS. Stitch to form six sections: Set 1–2¼" (5.7 cm) + Set 2 + Set 1–1¾" (4.4 cm). Stitch these to the 1¼" (3.2 cm) spacer of Fabric B. Trim. Rotate and stitch to a 1¼" (3.2 cm) spacers of Fabric D. Trim. Rotate and stitch edge to edge to the other 1¼" (3.2 cm) spacer of Fabric D. Trim.

BAND. Stitch the sections and alternating spacers B and E as shown. Cut through the spacers at a 45° angle, equidistant between seamlines. Rotate and stitch edge to edge as shown. Square off the ends by slicing through the section once and transferring the slice to the opposite end. Both ends will be square, forming the Desert Flower band.

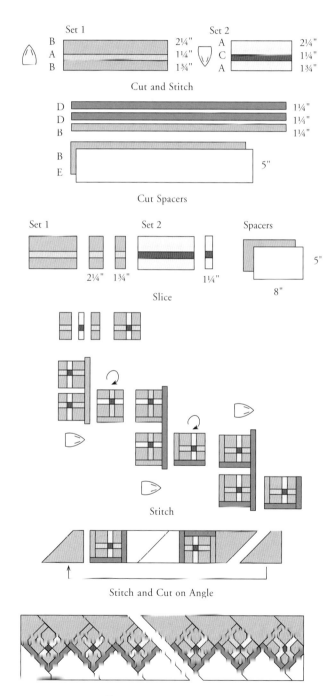

Cut and Stitch

Cut Spacers

Slice

Stitch

Stitch and Cut on Angle

Slice Band and Square Off

71

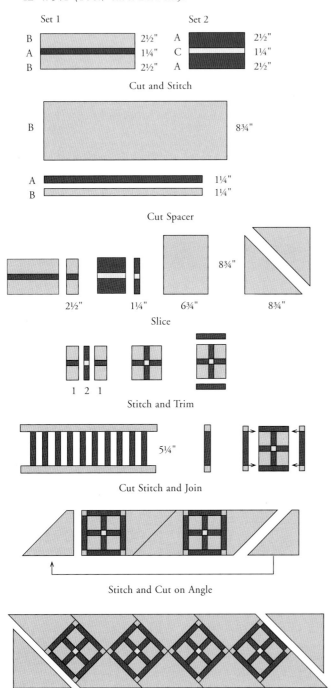

GREEK CROSS

Greek Cross is a pleasing, symmetrical design that can be very striking, depending on the colors and fabrics chosen. Tricky for beginners, the band requires great care in left/right placement and exact seams. Once sewn into a quilt, the band measures 42" x 9½"(106.7 cm x 24.1 cm).

Set 1

B	2½"
A	1¼"
B	2½"

Set 2

A	2½"
C	1¼"
A	2½"

Cut and Stitch

| B | 8¾" |

| A | 1¼" |
| B | 1¼" |

Cut Spacer

2½"　1¼"　6¾"　8¾"

Slice

1　2　1

Stitch and Trim

5¼"

Cut Stitch and Join

Stitch and Cut on Angle

Square Off

STRIP SETS. Cut three strips of fabric, each measuring at least 24" (61 cm), as follows:

> One 1¼" (3.2 cm) strip of Fabric A
>
> Two 2½" (6.4 cm) strips of Fabric B

Cut three strips, each at least 7" (17.8 cm):

> One 1¼" (3.2 cm) strip of Fabric C
>
> Two 2½" (6.4 cm) strip of Fabric A

For use as spacers, cut five strips selvage to selvage:

> Three 1¼" (3.2 cm) strips of Fabric A
>
> One 1¼" (3.2 cm) strip of Fabric B
>
> One 8¾" (22.2 cm) strip of Fabric B

Stitch together lengthwise to form two strip sets as shown.

SEGMENTS. Slice Set 1 into eight 2½" (6.4 cm) segments. Slice Set 2 into four 1¼" (3.2 cm) segments. Slice the 8¾" (22.2 cm) spacer strip into four 6¾"(17.1 cm) segments and one 8¾" x 8¾" (22.2 cm) square. Slice the square diagonally to make two triangles.

SECTIONS. Stitch the segments edge to edge as shown to form four sections: Set 1, Set 2, Set 1. Stitch these edge to edge to one of the 1¼" (3.2 cm) strips of Fabric A. Trim. Repeat with the opposite edge. Next, slice the remaining 1¼" (3.2 cm) strip of Fabric A into eight 5¼" (13.3 cm) pieces. Stitch them between the two selvage-to-selvage 1¼" (3.2 cm) strips of Fabric B. Trim. Join one of these to each side of each partial section to complete.

BAND. Stitch the sections edge to edge, alternating with spacer strip B as shown. Cut through the spacers at a 45º angle, equidistant between seamlines. Rotate and stitch edge to edge. Use the two triangles to square the edges and form the Greek Cross band.

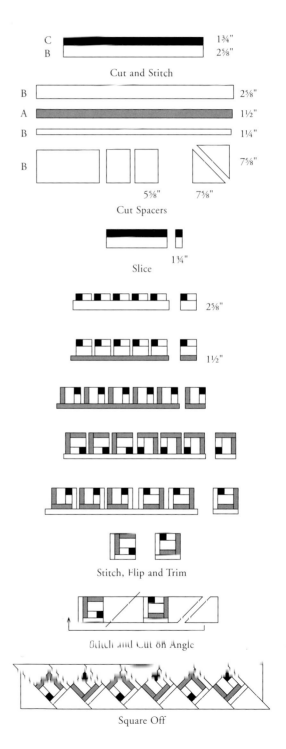

SPARKS & EMBERS

Rising and falling across the band, the V-shape provides an interesting accent in any Seminole quilt. Once sewn into a quilt, the band measures 42" x 9½" (106.7 cm x 24.1 cm).

STRIP SETS. Cut two strips of fabric, each measuring at least 11" (27.5 cm), as follows:

One 1¾" (4.4 cm) strip of Fabric C

One 2⅝" (6.7 cm) strip of Fabric B

For use as spacers, cut six more strips, selvage to selvage, as follows:

Two 1½" (3.8 cm) strips of Fabric A

Two 1¼" (3.2 cm) strips of Fabric B

One 2⅝" (6.7 cm) strips of Fabric B

One 7⅝" (20 cm) strips of Fabric B

Stitch the strips together lengthwise as shown to form a strip set. Cut the 7⅝" (20 cm) spacer strip of Fabric B into six 5⅝" (14.3 cm) segments and one 7⅝" (19.2 cm) square. Cut the square diagonally into two triangles. Set the other spacers aside.

SEGMENTS. Slice the strip set into six 1¾" (4.4 cm) segments.

SECTIONS. Stitch the segments to the 2⅝" (6.7 cm) strip of Fabric B. Trim. Stitch to one of the 1½" (3.8 cm) spacer strips of Fabric A. Trim. Flip and repeat, this time stitching to the second 1½" (3.8 cm) spacer strip of Fabric A. Trim. Stitch to one of the 1¼" (3.2 cm) spacer strips of Fabric B, flipping alternate sections as shown. Trim. Stitch to the second 1¼" (3.2 cm) spacer strip of Fabric B as shown. Trim.

BAND. Stitch the sections and alternating 7⅝" (20 cm) spacers of Fabric B edge to edge. Cut through the spacers at a 45° angle, equidistant between consecutive Rotate and stitch edge to edge, matching seamlines. Use the two triangles to square the edges and form band.

73

Chapter 7

ANGLE BANDS

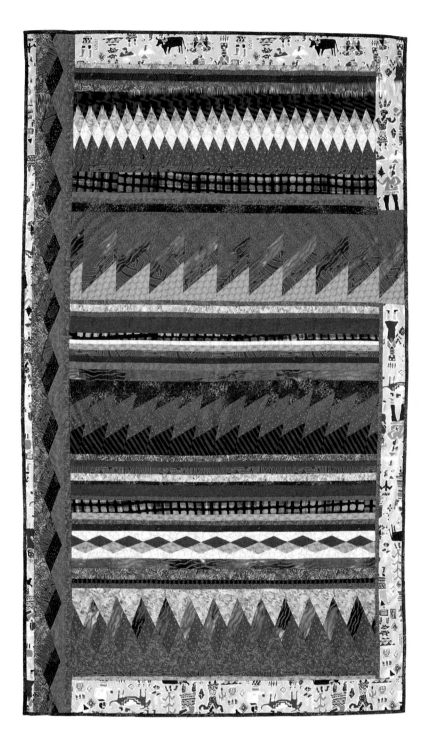

45" x 72" (114 cm x 183 cm)
From top: Spikes (angle); Diamonds variation (angle);
Diamonds variation (angle); Jagged Edge (angle);
Diamonds (angle); side bands: Chain (angle).

PEAKS

Peaks is the simplest of mirror-angle bands, a series of upside down Vs that run across the band. Despite its steady rhythm, the large scale of this band makes it stand out. Once sewn into a quilt, the band measures 42" x 7" (106.7 cm x 17.8 cm).

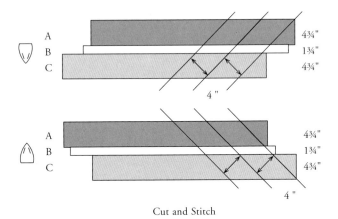

Cut and Stitch

STRIP SETS. Cut six strips of fabric, selvage to selvage, as follows:

> Two 4¾" (12.1 cm) strips of Fabric A
>
> Two 1¾" (4.4 cm) strips of Fabric B
>
> Two 4¾" (12.1 cm) strips of Fabric C

Stitch together lengthwise as shown to form two mirrored staggered strip sets.

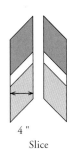

4"

Slice

SEGMENTS. Slice diagonally into 4" (10.2 cm) segments on a 45° angle.

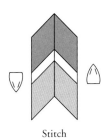

Stitch

SECTIONS. Stitch pairs of segments edge to edge, matching seamlines.

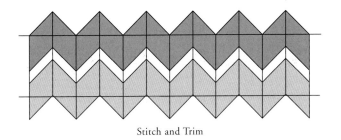

Stitch and Trim

BAND. Stitch the sections edge to edge, matching seamlines, to form the Peaks band. Trim.

A simple variation when making the sections is to flip alternate segments.

JAGGED PEAKS

A simple variation on Peaks, this mirror-angle band has a more staggered look, creating an irregular calypso rhythm and so attracting the eye. Once sewn into a quilt, the band measures 4" x 73½" (105.7 cm x 20.3 cm)

STRIP SETS. Cut eight strips of fabric, selvage to selvage, as follows:

     Two 4¾" (12.1 cm) strips of Fabric A

     Two 1¼" (3.2 cm) strips of Fabric B

     Two 1¼" (3.2 cm) strips of Fabric C

     Two 4¾" (12.1 cm) strips of Fabric D

Stitch together lengthwise as shown to form two mirrored staggered strip sets.

SEGMENTS. Slice diagonally into 4" (10.2 cm) segments on a 45° angle.

SECTIONS. Stitch pairs of segments edge to edge, matching seamlines and flipping alternate segments.

BAND. Stitch the sections edge to edge, matching seamlines. Trim to complete the Jagged Peaks band.

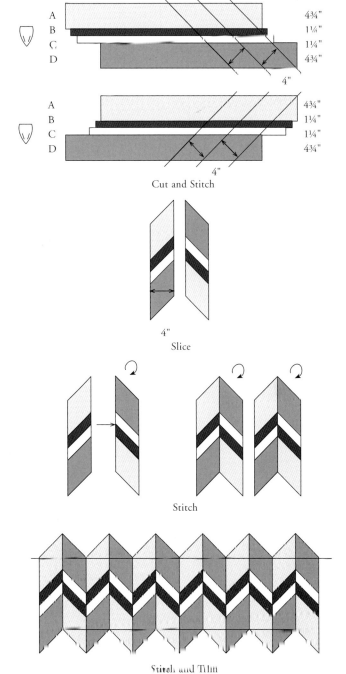

77

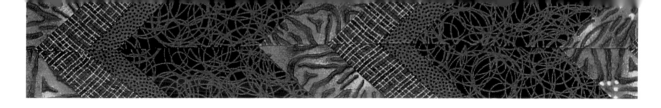

A R R O W H E A D

Quick and rhythmic, Arrowhead sweeps the eye across the quilt. Easy to make from four fabrics, this is one of the simplest yet most dramatic mirror-angle designs. Once sewn into a quilt, the band measures 35" x 2½" (88.9 cm x 6.4 cm).

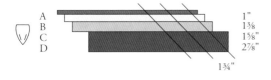

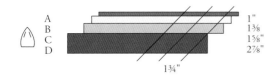

Cut and Stitch

STRIP SETS. Cut four strips of fabric, selvage to selvage, as follows:

> One 1" (2.5 cm) strip of Fabric A
> One 1⅜" (3.5 cm) strip of Fabric B
> One 1⅝" (4.1 cm) strip of Fabric C
> One 2⅞" (7.3 cm) strip of Fabric D

Cut the strips in half and stitch together lengthwise as shown to form two mirrored strip sets.

Slice

SEGMENTS. Slice diagonally on a 45° angle into 1¾" (4.4 cm) segments as shown.

Match Segments

SECTIONS. Stitch segments together into two sections as shown. Square off the ends by slicing through each section once and transferring the slice to the opposite end. Both ends will now be square. Try to slice in the same place on each section.

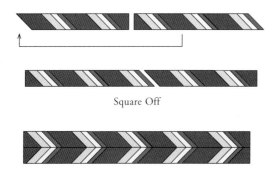

Square Off

Join

BAND. Join the sections edge to edge as shown, matching seamlines, to complete the Arrowhead band.

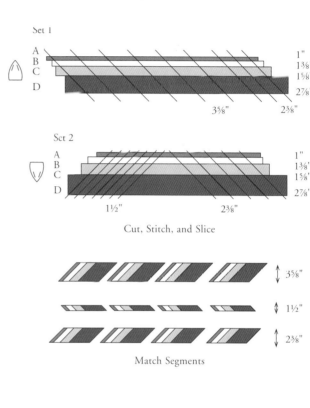

ZIG-ZAG

Reminiscent of the insignia of childhood hero, Zorro, Zig-zag is one of the most eye-catching Seminole designs. Depending on color placement it can easily be the centerpiece of a Seminole quilt. Once sewn into a quilt, the band measures 41" x 6" (104.1 cm x 15.2 cm).

STRIP SETS. Cut eight strips of fabric, selvage to selvage, as follows:

Two 1" (2.5 cm) strips of Fabric A

Two 1⅜" (3.5 cm) strips of Fabric B

Two 1⅝" (4.1 cm) strips of Fabric C

Two 2⅞" (7.3 cm) strips of Fabric D

Stitch together lengthwise as shown to form two strip sets.

Cut, Stitch, and Slice

SEGMENTS. Slice Set 1 diagonally on a 45° angle into six 3⅝" (9.2 cm) segments and two 2⅜" (6 cm) segments. Fold Set 2 and slice off the edges at a 45° angle. Open out and slice diagonally on a 45° angle into six 1½" (3.8 cm) segments from the left and four 2⅜" (6 cm) segments from the right.

Match Segments

SECTIONS. Stitch segments of equal width together edge to edge into three sections as shown. Square off the ends by slicing through each section once and transferring the slice to the opposite end. Both ends will now be square. Try to slice in the same place on all three sections.

Square Off

BAND. Join the sections edge to edge as shown, matching seamlines, to complete the Zig-zag band. Finger-press seams to interlock.

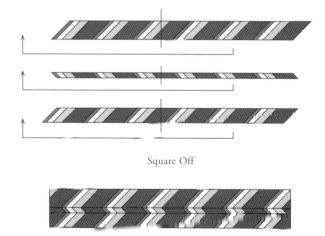

Join

79

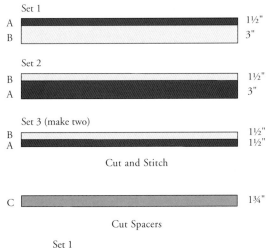

ARROW

A wonderfully versatile band in three colors, Arrow swiftly directs the eye to whatever part of the quilt the quilter wishes to highlight. It also looks pretty as a quilt border. Once sewn into a quilt, the band measures 40" x 7" (101.6 cm x 17.8 cm).

STRIP SETS. Cut eight strips of fabric, selvage to selvage, as follows:

Three 1½" (3.8 cm) strips of Fabric A

Three 1½" (3.8 cm) strips of Fabric B

One 3" (7.6 cm) strip of Fabric A

One 3" (7.6 cm) strip of Fabric B

Cut two 1¾" (4.4 cm) spacer strips of Fabric C. Stitch together lengthwise as shown to form three strip sets. Set the spacer strips aside.

SEGMENTS. Fold Set 1 and Set 2 end to end and slice diagonally on a 45° angle into 2½" (6.4 cm) segments. Without folding Set 3, and using the 3" (7.6 cm) ruler mark along the edge of the strip, slice diagonally on a 45° angle as shown, alternating cuts at 45° and 90° angles.

Measure, Cut, and Slice

SECTIONS. Match the segments from Set 1, Set 2, and Set 3 as shown and stitch.

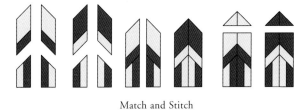

Match and Stitch

BAND. Trim each section, then join together with spacers between each section to complete the Arrow band. The arrows can point up, down, or across the quilt.

Join with Spacers

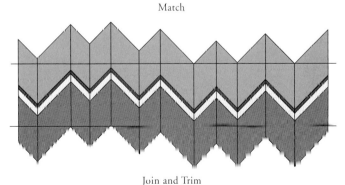

FRATERNAL PEAKS

One of the most complex mirror-angle designs, the uneven look of Fraternal Peaks makes it particularly exciting. Depending on color choices, the pattern can be bold and demanding, or quite subtle. Once sewn into a quilt, the band measures 42"x 8½" (106.7 cm x 21.6 cm).

STRIP SETS. Cut eight strips of fabric, selvage to selvage, as follows:

> Two 5" (12.7 cm) strips of Fabric A
> Two ⅞" (2.2 cm) strips of Fabric B
> Two 1-¼" (3.2 cm) strips of Fabric C
> Two 5" (12.7 cm) strips of Fabric D

Stitch together lengthwise to form two mirrored staggered strip sets as shown.

SEGMENTS. Slice Set 1 diagonally on a 45° angle into six segments measuring: 2-¾" (7 cm); 2-¾" (7 cm); 4" (10.2 cm); 4-⅞" (12.4 cm); 3" (7.6 cm); and 4-⅜" (11.1 cm). Slice Set 2 into six segments measuring: 4-¾" (12.1 cm); 2-¾" (7 cm); 3" (7.6 cm); 3-½" (8.9 cm); 3-⅞" (9.8 cm); and 4-¾" (12.1 cm).

SECTIONS. Stitch segments in the sequence shown, matching seamlines.

BAND. Trim the edges parallel, square to the seamlines, to form the Fraternal Peaks band.

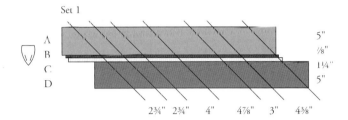

Set 1

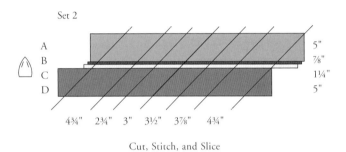

Set 2

Cut, Stitch, and Slice

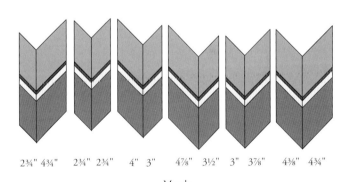

Match

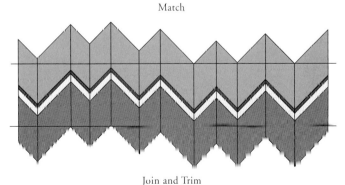

Join and Trim

CHAIN

A simple, repeating pattern in four colors, this open-angle band works well made in four fabrics as an decorative accent in any quilt. Chain and the three bands that follow are all made from the same strip set. Once sewn into a quilt, the band measures 38" x 3½" (96.5 cm x 8.9 cm).

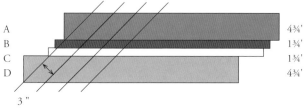

Cut, Stitch, and Slice

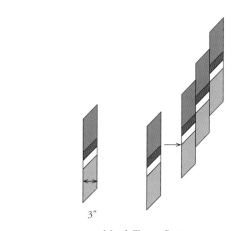

Match Top to Bottom

Stitch

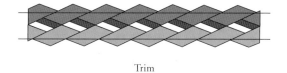

Slice and Square Off

STRIP SET. Cut four strips of fabric, selvage to selvage, as follows:

> One 4¾" (12.1 cm) strip of Fabric A
> One 1¾" (4.4 cm) strip of Fabric B
> One 1¾" (4.4 cm) strip of Fabric C
> One 4¾" (12.1 cm) strip of Fabric D

Stitch together lengthwise as shown.

SEGMENTS. Slice diagonally into seven 3" (7.6 cm) segments on a 45° angle.

SECTIONS. Stitch the segments edge to edge, matching the top seamline to the bottom seamline in the next segment as shown. To square off the ends, slice through the section once and transfer the slice to the opposite end, matching seamlines.

BAND. Turn the section on its side and trim to form the Chain band. Make sure the trimmed edges are parallel.

Trim

D I A M O N D S

Big and bold, Diamonds is one of the strongest Seminole designs. It easily takes center stage in a quilt. This open-angle band is easy to make using four fabric colors. Once sewn into a quilt, the band measures 41" x 10" (104.1 cm x 25.4 cm).

STRIP SET. Cut eight strips of fabric, selvage to selvage, as follows:

> Two 4¾" (12.1 cm) strips of Fabric A
>
> Two 1¾" (4.4 cm) strips of Fabric B
>
> Two 1¾" (4.4 cm) strips of Fabric C
>
> Two 4¾" (12.1 cm) strips of Fabric D

Stitch together lengthwise as shown to form two identical strip sets.

SEGMENTS. Slice diagonally into sixteen 3" (7.6 cm) segments on a 45° angle.

SECTIONS. Stitch the segments edge to edge, matching the bottom seamline in one segment to the top seamline in the next, as shown. To square off the ends, slice through the section once and transfer the slice to the opposite end, matching seamlines.

BAND. Trim to form the Diamond band. Make sure the trimmed edges are parallel.

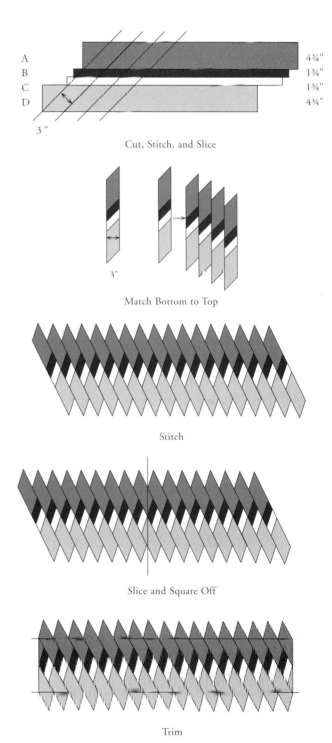

Cut, Stitch, and Slice

Match Bottom to Top

Stitch

Slice and Square Off

Trim

JAGGED EDGE

Jagged Edge is a strong, crisp repeating pattern. An open-angle band made with four fabrics, it is a good, strong accent band in any quilt. Once sewn into a quilt, the band measures 40" x 5" (101.6 cm x 12.7 cm).

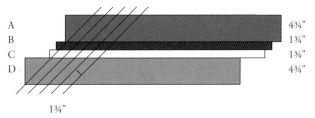

Cut, Stitch, and Slice

STRIP SET. Cut four strips of fabric, selvage to selvage, as follows:

> One 4¾" (12.1 cm) strip of Fabric A
> One 1¾" (4.4 cm) strip of Fabric B
> One 1¾" (4.4 cm) strip of Fabric C
> One 4¾" (12.1 cm) strip of Fabric D

Stitch together lengthwise as shown.

SEGMENTS. Slice diagonally into thirteen 1¾" (4.4 cm) segments on a 45° angle.

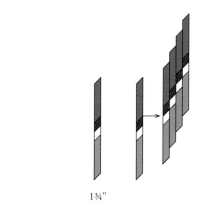

Match Top to Center

SECTIONS. Stitch the segments edge to edge, matching the top seamline in the first segment to the center seamline in the next, as shown. To square off the ends, slice through the section once and transfer the slice to the opposite end, matching seamlines.

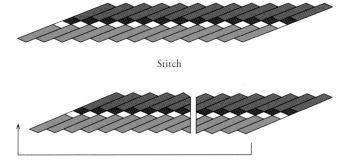

Stitch

Slice and Square Off

Trim

BAND. Turn the section on its side and trim to form the Jagged Edge band. Make sure the trimmed edges are parallel.

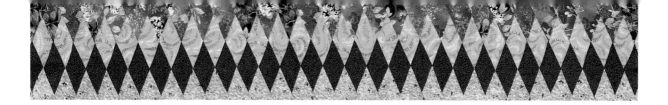

SPIRES

Graceful and elegant, the narrow diamonds in Spires are particularly eye-catching. It is made in the same way as the other open-angle bands. Once sewn into a quilt, the band measures 40" x 8" (101.6 cm x 20.3 cm).

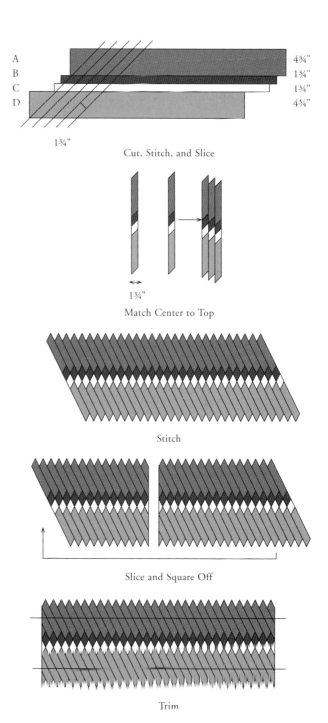

Cut, Stitch, and Slice

Match Center to Top

Stitch

Slice and Square Off

Trim

STRIP SET. Cut eight strips of fabric, selvage to selvage, as follows:

> Two 4¾" (12.1 cm) strips of Fabric A
> Two 1¾" (4.4 cm) strips of Fabric B
> Two 1¾" (4.4 cm) strips of Fabric C
> Two 4¾" (12.1 cm) strips of Fabric D

Stitch together lengthwise as shown to form two identical strip sets.

SEGMENTS. Slice diagonally into twenty-nine 1¾" (4.4 cm) segments on a 45° angle.

SECTIONS. Stitch the segments edge to edge, matching the center seamline in one segment to the top seamline in the next, as shown. To square off the ends, slice through the section once and transfer the slice to the opposite end, matching seamlines.

BAND. Turn the section on its side and trim to form the Spires band. Make sure the trimmed edges are parallel.

CRYSTALS

Intricate and elegant, this sensational open-angle band more than rewards the effort it takes to make. Once sewn into a quilt, the band measures 40"x 10" (101.6 cm x 25.4 cm).

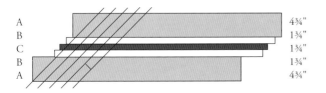

Cut, Stitch, and Slice

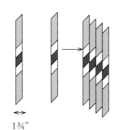

1¾"

Match Upper-Center to Top

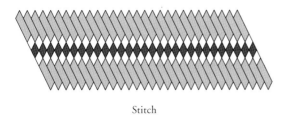

Stitch

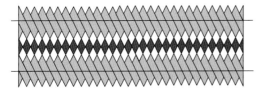

Slice and Square Off

STRIP SETS. Cut ten strips of fabric, selvage to selvage, as follows:

      Four 4¾" (12.1 cm) strips of Fabric A

      Four 1¾" (4.4 cm) strips of Fabric B

      Two 1¾" (4.4 cm) strips of Fabric C

Stitch together lengthwise as shown to form two identical strip sets.

SEGMENTS. Slice each set diagonally into twenty-nine 1¾" (4.4 cm) segments on a 45° angle.

SECTIONS. Stitch the segments edge to edge, matching the upper-center seamline in one segment to the top seamline in the next, as shown. To square off the ends, slice through the section once and transfer the slice to the opposite end, matching seamlines.

BAND. Turn the section on its side and trim to form the Crystals band. Make sure the trimmed edges are parallel.

Trim

S E R P E N T I N E

Smooth and easy, this pattern slinks along the band. Another open-angle pattern, Serpentine is bold enough to work as the centerpiece of a quilt, yet is also a graceful accent pattern. Once sewn into a quilt, the band measures 42" x 4" (106.7 cm x 10.2 cm).

STRIP SET. Cut five strips of fabric, selvage to selvage, as follows:

> Two 4¾" (12.1 cm) strips of Fabric A
> Two 1¾" (4.4 cm) strips of Fabric B
> One 1¾" (4.4 cm) strips of Fabric C

Stitch together lengthwise as shown.

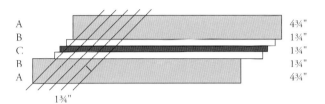

Cut, Stitch, and Slice

SEGMENTS. Slice diagonally into thirteen 1¾" (4.4 cm) segments on a 45° angle.

SECTIONS. Stitch the segments edge to edge, matching the top seamline in one segment to the upper-center seamline in the next, as shown. To square off the ends, slice through the section once and transfer the slice to the opposite end, matching seamlines.

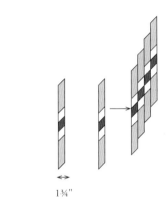

Match Top to Upper-Center

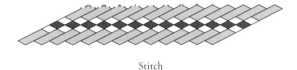

Stitch

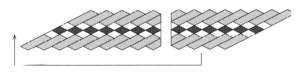

Slice and Square Off

BAND. Turn the section on its side and trim to form the Serpentine band. Make sure the trimmed edges are parallel.

Trim

Chapter 8

ASSEMBLING SEMINOLE
BANDS INTO QUILTS

40" x 54" (102 cm x 137 cm)
From top: Arrow variation (angle), Maze/Letter 1 (alternate);
Tumbling Cross (floating); Diamonds (straight)

Getting Started

Once the bands are complete, it's time for one of the most exciting and most challenging steps in making a Seminole quilt—bringing the bands together in a way that is interesting, arresting, and unique to you.

All the bands in *Simply Seminole* are designed to be assembled into quilts that will measure 45" (114.3 cm) wide. This does not mean that your bands must all measure 45" (114.3 cm), as variations from band to band will all be covered up by the quilt borders.

Seminole quilts are much easier and quicker to assemble and finish than traditional block quilts. There are four key steps. First, the bands and the plain horizontal strips are assembled in clusters. Next, these clusters of bands are simultaneously attached to the backing and batting and quilted. Although this saves time, it requires care and attention to make sure the final product is neat and well finished. Next, the vertical and horizontal borders are added. Finally the binding finishes off the quilt.

To begin assembly, first set up your work area. Hang a length of batting measuring 45" x 72" (114 cm x 183 cm) on an open wall space at eye level. I find a poly-core batting, such as Warm and Natural, works best, as its cohesive surface allows the bands to stay in place without pinning. To serve as a color guide, hang a piece of the fabric you wish to be dominant in your quilt next to the batting. This will be a useful reference as you begin selecting and placing bands.

Selecting and Placing Bands

One of the most exciting and enjoyable aspects of Seminole is seeing the individual bands you have worked on come together in a complete quilt. There are different ways of planning the final quilt. Some of us have it sketched out in our minds from the start and know exactly where we want each band to go. Others wait to see the finished bands before we decide final placement. For some of us, the fun of Seminole is in arranging and rearranging the bands for different effects.

Some of the most exciting Seminole quilts are created by combining bands from each category: alternate bands, stairstep bands, floating bands, and angle bands. This allows you to showcase your talents, providing variety and contrast within the same quilt.

Arrange the bands horizontally onto the batting. To begin, space at regular intervals, with equal space between the bands. You may later decide to vary the spacing as your quilt takes shape.

Visual Balance

To achieve what I call visual balance in placing the bands, there are two elements to keep in mind: balancing the design and balancing the color. To balance the design, try separating your bands into two design types: large scale and small scale. Avoid clustering bands of the same type into the same area of the quilt. Instead, space them regularly throughout. Go through the same exercise with diagonal and straight designs to avoid grouping all like bands together. Similarly, keep the overall look of the quilt in mind when placing bands of different colors. Separate them into darks and lights or into high and low contrasts. Distribute the colors evenly throughout the quilt.

More important than following any guidelines for good design when placing bands is to place them in a way that is visually appealing to you. The advice here

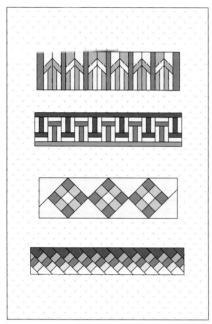

Placing the Bands

Placing Wide Horizontal Strips

is meant only as a checklist to help you get started and to help you identify problems when you feel that your design doesn't work as well as you'd like. The trick is to keep experimenting. Move the bands around and see how the quilt changes. Rearrange the colors, mix up the different band types. Keep the batting with bands in position up on the wall for several days or for as long as it takes for you to feel comfortable with the overall placement.

Once placement of the bands is complete, a good deal of batting will still show between and around them, as shown in the diagram.

PLACING HORIZONTAL STRIPS

The horizontal strips are those plain strips of unpieced fabric that serve to separate the Seminole bands in the quilt. They serve a dual purpose: to allow the eye to rest between bands and to reinforce color use within the bands. There are no rules on how to place the horizontal strips, but here's the process I usually follow.

1. Cut several wide strips of the fabric you wish to dominate the quilt and place between the bands. In the quilt pictured on page 89, I used a fun, novelty fabric cut to a 4¼" (10.8 cm) width.

2. Select the colors you wish to emphasize in your quilt and cut several narrower strips of these support fabrics. I chose the calming effect of pale greens and blues for the quilt on page 89, cut 1¾" (4.4 cm) wide. Place these adjacent to the wider horizontal strips in a way that is pleasing to you.

3. Select high-contrast fabrics that repeat contrast colors used in the bands. Cut narrow strips and place them next to the support strips. The 1" (2.5 cm) strips of red, yellow, and gold in the quilt on page 89 draw the eye into the quilt, yet because they are very narrow they do not overpower the bands. They give this quilt the lively, playful feel I wanted, but are restrained by placement next to the slightly wider pale green and blue strips.

Make sure you leave enough batting uncovered at the top and bottom of the quilt to allow space for the quilt border.

91

Placing Narrow Horizontal Strips

Stitching Assembly Sets

Placing High-Contrast Fabrics

JOINING BANDS AND HORIZONTAL STRIPS

Once you have decided the best placement of bands and horizontal strips in your quilt, it's time to begin sewing them together to form the quilt top. This is done several bands/strips at a time.

1. Beginning at the top of the quilt, remove each of the Seminole bands and the horizontal strips on either side of it from the batting. Each of these is an **assembly set.**

2. Match the bands/strips in each assembly set at one end. Stitch the top seam from left to right and the bottom seam from right to left. As the bands and strips in each assembly set will be of varying lengths, trim all to the length of the shortest in the set. Press all seams closed, pressing toward horizontal strips.

3. Following your original placement, stitch remaining horizontal strips into assembly sets until all are incorporated. As you work, alternate the direction of seams.

4. Reposition the finished assembly sets on the batting, pinning in place. Center each set on the batting, making sure that it is level and parallel to other sets.

ATTACHING THE BACKING

For quilts made from the bands in *Simply Seminole*, you will need 2¾ yards (7 meters) of backing fabric, cut selvage to selvage—approximately 40" to 42" (102 to 107 cm).

1. Cut the backing fabric in half lengthwise. Trim off the selvage edges. Stitch as shown so that the backing is wide enough for a 45" x 72" (114.5 cm x 182.9 cm) quilt. It should measure at least 47" x 75" (119.4 cm x 191 cm).

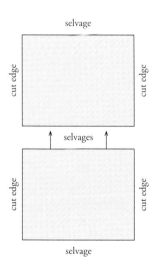

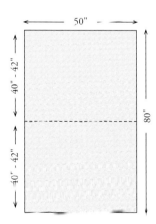

2. Spread the backing fabric wrong side up on a flat surface, such as a large table top or the floor. Smooth out the wrinkles.

3. Center the batting with the pinned assembly sets on top of the backing. Approximately 1" (2.5 cm) of backing should show on all sides. Smooth the batting, tugging the backing from underneath so that both lie flat.

4. Roll carefully from each end toward the center of the quilt, leaving the assembly set closest to the center exposed. Place on a flat work surface to begin assembly.

ASSEMBLY

1. Working on the band set nearest the center of the quilt, use a ruler to check that the top edge is straight and does not curve at the ends or bow in the center. Pin the top edge through all three layers—the assembly set, the batting, and the backing. Start pinning at the center and work out to the sides. Point the pin toward the assembly set, with the pin head extending over the batting. Smooth outward toward the edge. Place pins every 1½" (3.8 cm) to 2½" (6.4 cm). Align a ruler with the pinned edge and make a straight chalk line to the edge of the batting at either end of the assembly set. Repeat, this time pinning the bottom edge of the center assembly set.

2. Flip the top adjacent assembly set face down on top of the pinned set. Align the raw edges. Pin in the same way, this time through all four layers—the two assembly sets, the batting, and the backing. Position the pins in between those that were previously placed. Check that all layers remain smooth and taut between the two sets of pins with no puckers.

3. Flip the lower adjacent assembly set face down on top of the pinned center set. Align and pin as above.

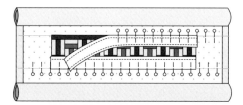

4. Beginning at the right edge of the batting and the top of the center set, stitch through all four layers—both assembly sets, the batting and the batting. Use a ¼" (0.6 cm) seam allowance. Stitch all the way across the sets to the left edge of the batting. Open out the set, smoothing the fabric right side up against the batting and backing. Check that the raw edge is parallel with the line of stitching.

5. Repeat, this time stitching the bottom of center set to the top of lower adjacent set. Three assembly sets are now stitched in place, forming a center block.

6. Repeat steps 1 to 5, adding new assembly sets to the center block of sets until all are stitched in place. Leave the top and bottom edges unsewn. After each row of stitching, check to make sure that the bands are straight and exactly parallel with each other.

As you stitch, it's easy for your seam lines to waver, curving up or down a little at the ends. As you add each band, make sure this doesn't happen. If the curve is slight, there's no need to rip out your seams. Instead, using a ruler and chalk marker, simply draw a line parallel to where the seam should have been. Use the chalk line instead of the raw edge of the assembly set as a stitching guide.

TOPSTITCHING WIDE BANDS

In bands that are wider than 6" (15 cm), such as Rattlesnake, you will need to topstitch in order to stabilize the band. You can either simply stitch in a

Topstitching

straight line through the center of the band across the quilt, or you can follow the pattern by stitching only on the seamlines. Smooth and pin the area to be stitched and remove the pins as you work across the band, from batting edge to batting edge.

ADDING BORDERS

The first step in choosing border fabric is to look again at the bands used in your quilt and decide which color or fabric you wish to dominate. Keep in mind that bands can take on an entirely different appearance depending upon the colors and fabrics used with them. Take time to experiment until you find the look that you like.

Similarly, border width is a matter of preference. Note, however, that if your bands are of varying widths, use the shortest band when you determine the width of your vertical borders. This way, the borders will cover up all the ragged edges of all the bands.

ADDING VERTICAL BORDERS

1. To determine vertical border placement, draw a chalk line down each side of the quilt. Make sure the ruler edge is even with the end of the narrowest assembly set and that the horizontal ruler markings align with the seamlines.

2. To determine the width of each border, measure the distance from the chalk line to the edge of the batting. Add ¾" (1.9 cm) to that measurement. To determine the length of the border, measure the distance from the top strip to the bottom strip. Add 1" (2.5 cm) to that measurement. Cut strips of border fabric to these dimensions.

3. Place the left border strip face down on the chalk line, with the border fabric extending into the body of the quilt, not toward the outer edge of the batting. Pin in place, starting at the center and working up and down the quilt. Sew from top to bottom of batting edges, with a ¼" (0.6 cm) seam allowance. Smooth open.

4. Pin and sew the right border in the same way.

ADDING HORIZONTAL BORDERS

1. Pin the unsewn horizontal edge at the top of the quilt to the batting and backing. Using a ruler, check that the vertical border seamline is square with this pinned edge. Make a chalk line along this top edge, out to the edges of the batting.

2. To determine the length of each border, measure from outer edge to outer edge. Width of the horizontal borders is a matter of preference. As in the quilt shown on page 89, I usually make the horizontal borders about 1" (2.5 cm) wider than the vertical borders. As you make more Seminole quilts, try experimenting with different border widths.

3. Lay the top border face down on the adjacent assembly set, aligning the edges. Pin between the previously placed pins and stitch, using a ¼" (0.6 cm) seam allowance. Remove pins and smooth outwards. Repeat with the bottom border. Check that vertical and horizontal borders are square. Trim excess batting and backing away.

Adding Vertical Borders

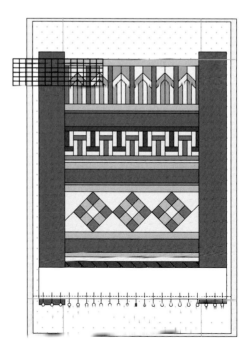

Adding Horizontal Borders

Adding Binding

Adding the binding is the last step in assembling the quilt. The fabric you choose may be one that is used in the quilt—perhaps as a secondary fabric or even as an accent. The binding frames the quilt, yet plays off the colors within it. Alternatively, you may choose an entirely new fabric that goes with the colors in your quilt. The technique is the same for Seminole as for any quilt style.

1. Measure each side of your quilt. Cut enough strips, 2" (5.1 cm) wide, selvage to selvage, to go round the entire quilt, plus an additional 6" (15 cm). Join the strips into one continuous piece of binding. To join, cut at a 45º angle at each end of each strip. Join end to end using the 45º angle to match strips in a straight line. This technique will spread the bulk so that the seams do not stack on top of each other when the binding is folded and sewn. Press all seams closed.

2. Fold in half lengthwise, wrong sides together, matching raw edges. Do not press.

3. Along the top of the quilt, align the raw edges of the folded binding with the raw edge of the quilt. Leave about 10" (25 cm) of the binding strip hanging free. Begin sewing about 25" (63.5 cm) from the bottom right-hand corner. Sew through all layers, using a ¼" (0.6 cm) seam allowance.

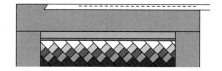

4. As you approach the first corner, stop sewing ¼" (0.6 cm) from the edge. Backstitch, then remove the quilt from the machine, leaving the threads intact. Fold the binding away from the quilt at a 45º angle, so that is aligned with the next side of the quilt.

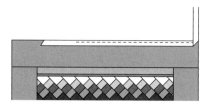

Fold back down so that the raw edge of the binding now matches the side of the quilt to be sewn and the fold in the binding lines up with the sewn edge, forming a miter. Sew through all layers. Continue around the quilt.

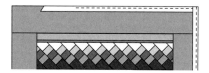

5. As you approach the 10" (25 cm) of loose binding, remove the quilt from the machine. Open the beginning and the end of the binding flat. Stretching the fabric slightly, place the end section on top of the beginning section, right sides up.

6. Using the edge of the end section as a guide, make a chalk line on the beginning section, marking the meeting point. Cut at a 45º angle ½" (1.3 cm) from the chalk line. (This allows for the two ¼" (0.6 cm) seam allowances needed to join the binding.)

7. Using the ½" (1.3 cm) seam allowance, join the beginning and end sections of the binding. Stitch right sides together.

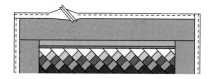

8. Press seam. Refold. Match edges and stitch for a continuous binding.

9. Turn the binding to the back and hand stitch in place.

10. As you come to the corners, fold to form a miter and stitch, continuing around the quilt.

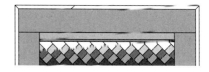

LESSON PLAN

45" x 72" (114 cm x 183 cm)
From top: Weave variation (floating); Letter H (alternate);
Syncopated Piano Keys variation (alternate);
Diamonds (angle); Fraternal Peaks (angle);
Syncopated Piano Keys (alternate); Dominoes (stairstep).

Classes built around *Simply Seminole* usually draw students with a wide range of sewing skills, as the techniques taught are appropriate for beginner, intermediate, and advanced quilters. Though some will catch on more quickly than others and work at a faster rate, it's possible to teach people of mixed abilities in the same class. Students learn not just from the instructor but, by sharing their work, from each other.

This lesson plan is based on three sessions of three hours each. Students will make a complete Seminole quilt made up or four or more band designs. You may also wish to include an additional first session on fabric selection. If a high portion of beginners sign up for the class, find some time at the first meeting to demonstrate and practice rotary cutting.

Each class period is arranged so that key techniques, which students may find difficult and require demonstration and practice, are presented first. This allows less experienced quilters the chance to observe others and finish the more complex work in class. Homework is based on less difficult techniques or on completing in-class assignments.

As they sign up for the class, encourage students to look through *Simply Seminole* and read Chapter 1.

SUPPLIES
Fabric (see page 39 for fabric requirements)
45" x 72" (114 cm x 183 cm) batting, preferably a polycore brand such as Warm and Natural
Rotary cutter
Cutting mat
6" x 24" (15 cm x 60 cm) ruler
Glass head quilting pins
Seam ripper
Chalk marker or marking pencil
Thread
Pencil and paper

FABRIC SELECTION CLASS

Particularly if there are a number of beginners in the class, it's a good idea to schedule an additional meeting to discuss and select fabric. Ask students to prepare by reading through Chapter 3 of *Simply Seminole*. Discuss aspects of color theory, particularly low, medium, and high contrast. Use Rattlesnake as an example of a band that requires varying degrees of contrast to be effective. Have students consider color contrast when selecting fabrics, arranging and rearranging different fabrics for differing levels of contrast.

CLASS 1

INTRODUCTION
Explain that Seminole bands fall into four types, based on key piecing techniques. During the classes, students will make one of each type: Alternate, Stairsteps, Floating, and Angle. Show a sample quilt with examples of each band type, or use the quilt photographed on page 11 to do this. (15 minutes)

Have students pin their battings to the wall and pin a strip of their main fabric alongside the batting.

INSTRUCTION
Introduce Stairsteps bands, explaining the key steps in making them (see page 14). Look over the instructions for making Harlequin on page 58. Have at least one sample available to show how the finished band looks. A sample using three colors and a symmetrical placement and a second sample using five colors would be helpful. Demonstrate each step in making the band, particularly the squaring off technique. Have the more advanced students in the class help beginners by demonstrating this technique one-on-one. As students complete their bands, have them press the bands to their batting to display. (1 hour)

Introduce Floating bands, explaining the key steps in making them (see page 15). Look over the instructions for making Tumbling Cross on page 68. Discuss how varying the color placement can result in bands that have a completely different look. Prepared samples with different color usage would be helpful. Look also at the several different samples of Tumbling Cross in the quilts photographed in *Simply Seminole*. Demonstrate how alternate seams are pressed in opposite directions so that the seam lines interlock. Piece the center section. Do not cut the spacer strip yet. (1 hour)

As students complete the pieced section of Tumbling Cross, have them pin several half-yard meter pieces of fabric to their batting and arrange the pieced sections on them. This will show the variety of looks they may achieve depending on the spacer fabric they select. (15 minutes)

Introduce Alternate bands, explaining the key steps in making them (see page 13). Look over the instructions for making Medallion/Letter I on page 54. Show at least two samples of finished bands, one in which color use makes the Letter I shape stand out, the other in which the Medallion shape is emphasized. Use these examples to introduce students to the concept of figure and ground, as discussed on page 36. (15 minutes)

HOMEWORK
By the next class students should have completed Harlequin, the pieced sections of Tumbling Cross, and Letter I/Medallion. Ask students to re-read the section on making Angle bands on page 16 and to look over the different designs on pages 76 to 87. Read Chapter 8.

CLASS 2

SHOW AND TELL
Have students pin their battings with attached bands and their selected main fabric to the wall. Compare differences in appearance created by color placement, particularly in the Medallion/Letter I bands. Ask students whether the colors in their bands are working out as they had planned. Have them decide which colors to emphasize in their next bands. Do they want to downplay certain colors or bring in new ones? How well do the colors work with their selected main fabric? Have students make suggestions on each other's work. (15 to 30 minutes)

INSTRUCTION
Introduce Angle bands, explaining the key steps in making them (see page 16). Look over the instructions for making Chain, Diamonds, Jagged Edge, and Spires (see pages 82 to 85). Explain that all four bands begin with identical strip sets and are cut in the same way: Chain and Diamonds into 3" (7.6 cm) segments; Jagged Edge and Spires into 1¾" (4.4 cm) segments. Jagged Edge and Chain require one strip set, Diamonds and Spires two sets.

Bring a prepared strip set and demonstrate using the ruler angle marking to cut 45° angles. You may need to demonstrate this more than once. Have the students stitch their sets. Encourage them to experiment with placement before sewing segments together. Beginning students may want to make Chain since it only uses seven segments to form the band, and so requires much less time to make. Press the bands to the batting as completed. (1 hour, 15 minutes)

Have students look again at their previously pieced sections of Tumbling Cross. Noting the colors in their completed bands, have them make a final selection of spacer fabric. Demonstrate how spacer strips are cut and have students complete Tumbling Cross. (45 minutes)

Once students have attached all four completed bands to their batting, discuss overall color usage in their quilts. Discuss the concept of visual balance (see page

90). Let students arrange their bands until they are satisfied with placement.

Look over the instructions for Syncopated Piano Keys on page 49. Explain that this is an easy-to-make design that can be used to bring together small quantities of each key color in a single band. Students may wish to use this simple band to accent the colors in the more complex bands and so help pull their quilts together.

Introduce horizontal strips. Have students begin cutting horizontal strips of main, supporting, and contrast fabrics. Press the strips to the batting. Rearrange and experiment with color placement.

Explain and demonstrate how to begin quilt assembly by identifying assembly sets and stitching them together (see page 92). Explain the importance of pinning assembly sets to batting so that they are level and parallel, as well as centered. (30 to 45 minutes)

HOMEWORK
Finish all bands, including Syncopated Piano Keys, if desired. Establish band and horizontal strip placement, and pin into place on the batting. Begin stitching assembly sets.

Re-read the section on adding binding in Chapter 8 (page 95). To practice binding in the next class, prepare a "fabric sandwich," made up of a 6"x 8" (15.2 cm x 20.3 cm) rectangle of batting, a piece of top fabric, and a piece of backing.

CLASS 3

SHOW AND TELL
Have students pin their batting with attached assembly sets (or uncompleted assembly sets and horizontal

strips) to the wall. Have students discuss each of the quilts and compare how each has evolved from the same four band designs. (15 to 30 minutes)

INSTRUCTION
Demonstrate layering the batting with pinned assembly sets on top of the backing piece (see page 93). Demonstrate assembly: pinning, flipping and stitching. Emphasize the importance of using the ruler to keep work squared and clean. Students may then proceed at their own pace, either joining more assembly sets or beginning assembly. Have students begin stitching assembly sets closest to center of quilt first. This way, even those students who work slowly will get to assemble at least two assembly sets while in class. (1 hour, 45 minutes)

Look over the instructions on adding the borders on page 94, and explain how to add vertical and horizontal borders. Some students may need to complete these at home. (15 minutes)

Look over the instructions on adding binding. Demonstrate and have students use their prepared rectangles to practice adding binding. (30 minutes)

HOMEWORK
Complete assembly sets and stitch to batting and backing. Complete borders and add binding.

Try to arrange a time when students can meet to show off their finished Seminole quilts!

A LAST MESSAGE
FROM THE AUTHOR

Having come to quilting from an art rather than sewing background, the most exciting part of quilting for me is making color and fabric choices. Seminole strip piecing gives me the freedom to concentrate on the aspects of quilting I enjoy the most. The speed and ease of the techniques mean that I can make quilts and try out new ideas almost as quickly as I can come up with them. I hope you have enjoyed working from *Simply Seminole* and that you take from it—as well as many beautiful quilts—skills you can apply to other quilting styles.

Dorothy Hanisko
Seattle, WA